Sausag

Other Cookbooks by A. D. Livingston

Cast-Iron Cooking

Grilling, Smoking, and Barbecuing

Cold-Smoking & Salt-Curing Meat, Fish, & Game

Good Vittles

Complete Fish & Game Cookbook

Venison Cookbook

Wild Turkey Cookbook

Bass Cookbook

Trout Cookbook

Saltwater Fish Cookbook

Duck and Goose Cookbook

Sausage

A. D. Livingston

THE LYONS PRESS
Guilford, Connecticut
An imprint of The Globe Pequot Press

Published by The Globe Pequot Press
Previously published by The Lyons Press

The Lyons Press is an imprint of The Globe Pequot Press.

A few of the recipes used in this book were adapted from the author's cooking column for *Gray's Sporting Journal*. Acknowledgments to other authors and books are made in the text as appropriate.

Design by Joel Friedlander, Marin Bookworks
Illustrations by Jonathan Milo

Library of Congress Cataloging-in-Publication Data

Livingston, A.D., 1932–
    Sausage / by A.D. Livingston.
        p.   cm.
    Includes index.
    ISBN 1-55821-526-3
    1. Cookery (Sausages). 2. Sausages. 3. Cookery, International. I. Title.
TX749.5.S28L58 1998
641.6'6—dc21   97-17151
                                                                                          CIP

Manufactured in the United States of America
First edition/Third printing

Contents

Introduction

Tasty sausage can be made with an inexpensive hand-cranked meat grinder, a chunk of fresh pork, and a few readily available spices. Because the process is so easy, I decided to start this book off by actually making and cooking sausage in the first chapter, hopefully whetting the appetite instead of bogging down for a hundred pages in techniques and meat-curing formulae.

In subsequent chapters, we'll be stuffing good country sausage into casings, smoking and drying the links, and globe-trotting for recipes, sampling, along the way, surprisingly modern sausages from ancient Rome as well as tantalizing new flavors from Thailand.

Most of the recipes in this book are designed for using a total of ten pounds of meat. It's easy to scale the recipe up or down, but remember that the setup and cleanup time required to grind and stuff the meat will be the same for one pound or ten pounds. Besides, home-made sausage is so good that ten pounds goes pretty fast. Also, many homes have an extra freezer these days, making the large batch even more practical.

The "servings" recommended by most modern cookbooks have always bothered me. I suppose that some guide is needed, but far too many people have been left hungry by some recipes and serving rec-ommendations in modern cookbooks and magazines. How much sausage you eat depends on you and your requirements, tastes, and capacity, as well as, I think, on the occasion. As a rule, however, sausage is highly spiced and quite filling, so that those people who like half a pound of meat will probably find that a quarter pound of sausage will do. In this book, the recipes for the various sausages (usually presented under centered headings) do not offer advice on the number of servings. Recipes for various dishes that call for sausage as an ingredient, or for cooking sausage in some special way, may or may not offer serving sizes.

—A. D. Livingston

Easy Sausages

If you like to know what you are eating, have your sausage meat prepared at home or by some one whom you can trust.

—*Boston Cooking School Cook Book*, 1884

Good sausage starts with good meat. It's true that sausage is traditionally made with scraps from the butchering process, but they should at least be good scraps. Of course, you can also use prime cuts of meat in sausage, provided that the fat content is adjusted, and I've know rural practitioners who bragged about using entire hams or even the whole hog for sausages. If you make your own, the choice is yours. You also have more control of the fat content and chemical additives.

Of course, the complete sausage maker will want to grind his own meats. This process is discussed later in this chapter, along with equipment and meat-grinding tips. Right now, let's put together a simple sausage and cook some recipes just to show how easy it is.

Simple Sausage

The ingredient list for this recipe calls for ground lean pork and ground pork fat. Anyone who isn't proficient in the fundamentals of meat grinding should read the chapter through, or perhaps get a butcher to grind the meat.

7 pounds ground lean pork

3 pounds ground pork fat

4 tablespoons salt

2 tablespoons crushed dried sage

2 tablespoons freshly ground black pepper

1 tablespoon red pepper flakes

Thoroughly mix the ground meat, fat, and seasonings. Shape a thin patty and fry it in a hot skillet. Taste for seasonings. Add a little more sage, black pepper, or red pepper flakes to the mix if you want to make it hotter or change the flavor. Either cook the meat right away, refrigerate it for a day or two, or freeze it.

Storing Bulk Sausage

Bulk sausage should be cooked right away or frozen. If properly made from good meat, it will keep for several days in the refrigerator, but freezing it is the better choice.

Freezing Patties. I often make sausage patties from bulk sausage, wrap them with plastic film, and freeze them for future use. The sausage should also be labeled so that you'll know what they are and when they were made. Instead of labeling individually, I write the information on a freezer-proof plastic container and pack the patties in it for storage. This method helps keep things straight, and helps you find the small patties a month or two later.

The patties can be unwrapped and cooked in a skillet or on a griddle without prior thawing.

Freezing by the Pound. In addition to patties, I freeze bulk sausage in 1-pound units. These are wrapped in plastic film, wrapped again in freezer paper or aluminum foil, and labeled. I also freeze them in small freezer-proof plastic boxes that hold 1 cup each, packed tightly and capped with a little water. These are easy to thaw out in a microwave.

Larding Sausage Patties. Before the days of mechanical refrigeration, sausage patties were fried in lard on hog-killing day. The lard, of course, was rendered on the scene from pork fat. (Frying chunks of fat yielded lard and a delicacy known as cracklings, which, contrary to some modern cookbooks, are not merely fried pork skins.) The sausage patties were fried in the bubbling lard and packed into stone crocks. Then hot lard was poured in, completely covering the patties. As it cooled, the lard turned to a paste. The patties were dug out and reheated as needed. These patties were delicious, and are just as good today. The crock must be kept in a cool place, such as in an old-time springhouse or a modern refrigerator.

Cooking Bulk Sausage

In addition to being shaped into patties and cooked for breakfast in a skillet or on a griddle, bulk sausage can be used in meatballs, spaghetti sauce, pizza toppings, and so on, as well as in a variety of other recipes. Here are some of my favorites.

Easy Sausage Casserole

1½ pounds bulk sausage
8 hard-boiled chicken eggs, sliced
1 can condensed mushroom soup (10¾-ounce size)
2 cups grated Cheddar
½ cup bread crumbs
salt and pepper, to taste

Brown the sausage in a skillet, cooking until done, and drain. Place the sliced eggs into a large buttered casserole dish. Distribute the sausage evenly over the eggs, then spread with the soup. Mix cheese and bread crumbs; sprinkle over the dish. Bake in the oven long enough to heat the casserole through, then brown under the broiler. Season with salt and pepper to taste.

Mississippi Casserole

This old Mississippi dish calls for a combination of oysters and bulk sausage. It's hard to beat for texture and flavor, especially if you can gather your own fresh oysters. I cook it from time to time when I go oystering, or when I purchase a bag of fresh Apalachicola oysters.

2 pounds bulk sausage
2 pints freshly shucked oysters, drained
3 cups uncooked brown rice
2 cups chopped onion
2 cups chopped celery with tops
1 cup chopped fresh parsley or cilantro (divided)

Cook the rice by the directions on the package. Preheat the oven to 350 degrees F. Brown the sausage in a skillet, then pour the drippings into a saucepan or another skillet. Sauté the onion and celery in the sausage drippings for 10 minutes. In a bowl, mix the rice, sausage, onion, celery, ½ cup of the parsley, and all the oysters. Turn the mixture into a casserole dish and sprinkle with the rest of the parsley. Bake for 30 minutes. Feeds 6 to 10.

Sausage 'n' Two-Soup Casserole

This dish, like many other American casseroles, makes easy use of canned soups. It's very good. I like it with hot country sausage, made with plenty of red pepper flakes.

1 pound highly seasoned bulk sausage
1 can cream of chicken soup (10¾-ounce size)
1 can cream of mushroom soup (10¾-ounce size)
1 cup uncooked long-grain rice
1 can bamboo shoots (8-ounce size)
1 can water chestnuts (8-ounce size)
½ cup chopped red bell pepper
¼ cup chopped onion

¼ cup chopped celery with tops
salt

Preheat the oven to 350 degrees F. Grease a casserole dish, preferably one suitable for serving. Mix all the ingredients, spread in the dish, cover, and cook for 45 minutes. Feeds 4 as a main dish, or 8 as a side dish.

♪ Sausage Fingers

Here's an easy way to make finger food from bulk sausage. It's best to grate your own cheese instead of buying packaged shredded cheese. These are especially good, to me, when made with a rather hot sausage.

2 pounds bulk sausage
4 cups biscuit mix
10 ounces grated sharp Cheddar

Preheat the oven to 350 degrees F. Mix the ingredients, shape into fingers, place on a rack in a baking pan, and cook for 15 to 20 minutes. Serve warm.

♪ Crown Roast with Sausage Stuffing

This beautiful and tasty dish requires a crown roast of pork. Your butcher can prepare this for you. The chine bone should be removed, making the roast easy to carve at the table, and the roast should be joined at the ends, making a round presentation.

Sausage Stuffing

1 pound bulk sausage
4 cups French bread cubes
1½ cups chicken stock or broth (divided)
1 cup chopped onion
1 cup chopped celery
½ cup chopped walnuts
1 tablespoon cooking oil

Heat the oil in a large skillet. Sauté the sausage meat until lightly

7

browned, then stir in the onion, celery, and walnuts. Cook for a few minutes. Stir in ½ cup of the chicken stock. Simmer for 15 minutes, stirring and adding a little more stock as needed. Place the meat mixture into a large bowl, then mix in the bread crumbs and the remaining chicken stock. The stuffing can be refrigerated for a few hours, but it's best to use it immediately.

The Roast

1 crown roast, 7 to 12 pounds
juice of 1 lemon
1 teaspoon freshly ground black pepper
½ teaspoon granulated garlic
salt, to taste
stuffing (from above)

Record the weight of the roast. Preheat the oven to 350 degrees F. Place the roast into a well-greased shallow roasting pan. Mix the garlic, pepper, and salt into the lemon juice. Brush the juice mixture over the roast. Stuff the roast with the sausage mix. Place a strip of aluminum foil over the stuffed roast, being sure to cover the exposed bones at the top. Bake for 25 minutes per pound of meat, or until done. (If in doubt, cut into the roast; when done, the juices will not be bloody. Or use a meat thermometer, which should read at least 150 degrees F.) Remove the roast to a heated serving platter and let it cook a little longer from its own heat while you prepare the gravy.

The Gravy

2 tablespoons flour
pan drippings from roast
salt and pepper, to taste
4 cups water

Remove the rack from the roasting pan. Measure 2 tablespoons of the pan drippings, putting it into a saucepan or skillet. Heat the drippings and slowly stir in the flour, cooking and stirring over low heat for 15 minutes or longer. Pour off most of the remaining grease from the baking pan, then place the pan over two stove burners, and stir in the water along with some salt and pepper. Bring to a light boil, scraping up the pan dredgings with a spatula. Using pot holders, carefully tip the pan and pour about ½ cup of the liquid into the flour mixture. (If you prefer, dip up the hot liquid with a large spoon.) Turn up the heat on the saucepan and pour in a little more liquid, stirring as you go. Pour and stir until all the pan drippings have been blended into the saucepan. You should now have a nice gravy. Thin with a little more water if needed. Place the gravy into a serving dish.

Serve the gravy with the roast and stuffing, along with boiled or steamed cauliflower, snap beans, pickled crab apples, and plenty of French bread.

Don't forget that sausage patties are easy to cook on a griddle or in a skillet, and don't require cooking oil because some of the fat in the mix will cook out. These patties can be served for breakfast with eggs and toast and perhaps sliced tomatoes. Also, a great American classic requires nothing but a sausage patty sandwiched in biscuit halves. No mayonnaise or gravy or other condiments are needed.

Additional bulk sausage dishes are set forth in other chapters of this book under the recipes for specific sausages, such as chorizo or kielbasa.

Pork for Sausage

In spite of the direction of contemporary winds, pork has always been and still is, from a purely culinary viewpoint, the best all-around meat for sausage. Since the fat is not marbled in the flesh (as it is in beef), pork can be very lean, if properly chosen and well trimmed. On the other hand, sausage needs some fat. It really does. This fact makes fatty scraps of pork, trimmed out during the butchering process, a good choice for making sausage. Of course, such scraps were traditionally used for making home sausages at hog-killing time, usually during the first cool snap in autumn. If you butcher your own hogs, then by all means use scraps. But hog-killing day is for the most part a thing of the past, and these days even those people who raise their own pork usually take it on the hoof to a meat processor. Modern farmers and farm wives don't want to get their hands in it, and even some hog farmers and chicken farmers call themselves "producers."

The amount of fat in many sausage recipes is as high as 50 percent, and my guess is that most commercial sausages contain 50 percent or more. The home practitioner can cut back considerably, making a sausage that doesn't shrink drastically when cooked. The stickler for exact numbers can separate the fat and lean, then mix by weight as desired. It's easier, however, to use such cuts as the pork shoulder, which will contain about 25 to 30 percent fat. The fat content of these cuts will vary from pig to pig, and the trend these days is toward a leaner meat. In any case, using all the fat and lean meat from a shoulder will usually give a pleasing ratio of lean to fat. Of course, hams or hindquarters can also be used, but these will often be more expensive.

The pork shoulder is sometimes butchered and sold as one chunk, but it is usually divided into two main pieces, plus the shank and trotter. The butt, or Boston butt, is the big end, and is often marketed boned or semi-boned. I buy them bone-in because I like to make soup and provide a treat for my dog, Nosher. The picnic looks like a small ham. A little meat can be trimmed from the shank, but I like to save this piece for soups and stews, used along with the bones from the butt and picnic.

In addition to the shoulder, other parts of the pig can be used—even the very lean and more expensive loin and tenderloin cuts. It's fun, I think, to purchase a whole pig and reduce it to sausage. The term *whole-hog sausage* implies a superior product, giving you at least a psychological edge when serving sausage to your family and friends. Good meat really does help.

If you don't raise your own pigs or purchase them on the hoof from a farmer, your best bet is to gain the confidence of a good butcher. Tell him or her what you want and why. Some large supermarkets will provide good fresh meat because the turnover is high, but in many cases the personal touch and consumer confidence is missing, at least with this customer. Moreover, my experience with frozen meats purchased from supermarkets has been unpleasant. I don't want meat that has been displayed until the date of sale expires, then wrapped (or rewrapped) and

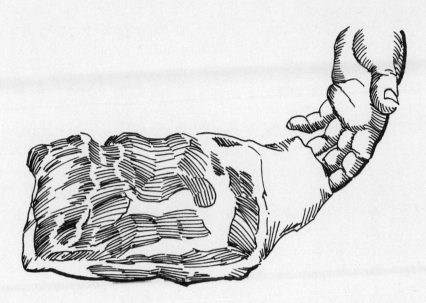

Picnic and Boston Butt

frozen. If such meats were thawed, cooked, and eaten right away, they might be all right. Not ideal, but all right. But when made into a large batch of sausage, it might well be stored in the refrigerator for several more days or even longer if cased and cured.

Most sausages are made with fresh pork instead of cured hams or other cured parts. The meat may be cured (salted down) during the sausage-making process, but it almost always starts out as fresh pork or fresh frozen pork. The fresher the better, I think. Of course, any fresh pork can carry the parasitic roundworm known as trichina, which is the culprit of trichinosis. This parasite can be killed by heating the pork to an internal temperature of 140 degrees F or thereabouts during the cooking process. It can also be destroyed in the raw pork by freezing it at 5 degrees F or less for thirty days. Freezing at colder temperatures shortens the time requirement, but most sausage makers working with home freezers will probably want to stick to the thirty days—and use a reliable thermometer.

Pork that has been properly frozen for the required length of time is said to be certified. Certified pork may also be purchased from your butcher. If readily available from a reliable source, it can save you some time. I hate to repeat this term in every pork recipe in this book, but I like to use it in any sausage that calls for pork. Sausages that are made and cooked or frozen right away can be made with uncertified pork, but they should be cooked thoroughly. Any sausage that is cured, smoked, or dried should be made with certified pork.

Salmonella is always a threat, especially with poultry and meats that have been run through a batch process. It can be controlled by cleanliness, proper refrigeration, and thorough cooking. Other problems—mainly bacterial toxin buildup—come about during curing and smoking and are discussed in subsequent chapters.

Other Sausage Meats

Although pork is the traditional sausage meat, until modern times the pig wasn't widely eaten outside Europe and China. Nomadic peoples—the Arabs, the Mongols, the Lapps, the American Plains Indians—really didn't care much for pork and might well have used other animals, such as camels or yaks or reindeer or aardvarks, for making sausage. The Mongols considered a fondness of pork to be a sure sign of "going Chinese," and they, or perhaps the ancient Scythians, might well have been the source of *kazy,* a modern-day Russian sausage made with horse meat. Also, the Scythians are known (if we may trust Herodotus) to have stuffed horse meat into a stomach, like Scotland's sheep haggis (Chapter 8), and cooked it over a low-smoke campfire made or perhaps sustained with the aid of horse bones.

Of course, the Germans also love pork (even more than the French do) and today the *wurstmachers* offer more than fifteen hundred kinds of sausage. Whether for domestic use or export, the German *wurst* must be made with pure meat—no fillers or extenders, chemical additives, or colorings. Don't ask what's in an American-made supermarket frank-furter these days.

In any case, pork isn't the only meat that can be used in sausages. Other chapters offer recipes and tips for working with chicken, turkey, beef, veal, lamb, game of all sorts, variety meats, such as liver, and even fish.

Often, the use of other meats instead of pork won't really alter the taste of the final product very much, especially with such highly seasoned sausages as chorizo. But often the texture and the color will be altered considerably.

Preparing the Meat

Here are a few steps and tips that will make it easier to grind sausage meat and hamburger.

1. Chilling or freezing the meats. Cold or partly frozen meats are easier to cut and grind—and they are safer to use because bacterial growth is greatly retarded at temperatues below 40 degrees F.

2. Trimming the meats. Trimming the meats of sinews prior to grinding can be very, very important. Tough, stringy tissue clogs up the meat grinder, making frequent cleaning necessary. Some of the tissue can be cut out in sheets while you trim the meat. A small, sharp fillet knife works well. Thorough trimming should be a part of cutting the meat into large segments and then into smaller chunks suitable for grinding.

3. Cutting the meat into chunks. Use a sharp knife to reduce the meat to chunks suitable for feeding into a sausage mill. I like mine about 1 inch square. Some people use strips of meat, but I cut mine across the grain to minimize the tissue problem. In other words, it's always best to cut the meat so that the tissue is not fed into the grinder in long strings.

   Usually, when cutting fatty pork such as Boston butts, I chunk the fat right along with the meat, trying to give a good mix. (Exceptions to this practice are pointed out in a few recipes in subsequent chapters.)

   It's best to keep the chunks of meat cold. If you are a slow worker or have lots of meat to cut, devise some way to keep the meat on ice. I use a large plastic tray with ice spread over the bottom, then I put the meat into a similar tray and place it nesting on top.

4. Mixing the meat. If using more than one kind of meat, or with a meat and fat ground separately, I usually mix them equally on a work surface within easy reach of the meat grinder, or in a large plastic tray. The tray is especially useful when the meat (or meats) is to be cured in the refrigerator before grinding, and the maximum size of the tray should be determined by the width and depth of your refrigerator interior.

5. Mixing the spices. Normally, I mix all the dry spices and salts, then sprinkle them evenly over the chunks of meat prior to grinding. It is important that the spices be evenly mixed and evenly distributed. This is especially important if the spices contain a cure such as saltpeter or sodium nitrite. (These cures are discussed in Chapter 3.)

In some recipes, other ingredients, such as bread crumbs or diced onions, are added at this point. In other recipes, these ingredients are mixed in after the meat has been ground.

6. Grinding the meat. Grind the meats while they are still very cold. If the meats have been properly cleaned, the grinding operation should go smoothly and quickly, although the plate and knife of the grinder may have to be cleaned along the way. To make sure all is well, keep an eye on the meat being extruded from the plate. If things clog up inside, you'll notice a reduced "flow." If you keep on grinding, the meat will be mashed and pulverized instead of cut and it will start to back up along the rotor. With a little practice, you'll be able to spot trouble early. A lot depends on your equipment, discussed below.

7. Adding other ingredients. Recipes vary, but liquids such as water and wine along with minced fresh onions and perhaps bread crumbs are usually mixed in after the meat has been ground. Use your hands.

After grinding, the mixture is usually stuffed into casings (Chapter 3) or treated as bulk sausage. In a few recipes, the ground meat is put into the refrigerator for a day or two to "cure" or to blend the flavors.

The Meat Grinder

Any good meat grinder or mincer can be used to make sausage, but a meat grinder with fine, medium, and coarse plates is highly desirable. Most of these also have several plates and sausage-stuffing tubes available as accessories. Never buy a sausage mill unless such accessories and spare parts are available.

Several mechanical and electrical meat grinders are marketed. I use the old-fashioned kind, covered below.

Hand-Cranked Meat Grinders

Usually made of plated cast iron, these grinders are available in several sizes. The small size will be satisfactory and may even be preferable for home kitchen production, owing to the simple mounting system, as explained below.

Mounting. Some sausage mills attach to the table or countertop with a suction cup, but these are not stable enough to be satisfactory. Others are mounted with four bolts. While this is indeed a superior mounting system, remember that the four bolts require four holes in your table or countertop. Never buy one of these unless you want to drill holes in your work surface.

The clamp-on meat grinder, which attaches to a flat surface with a hand screw and pressure plate, is better suited for easy use in most kitchens. Even so, this device won't fit easily onto some countertops or tables.

Clearly, the prospective sausage maker should consider the mounting systems before purchasing a meat grinder.

The Handle and the Auger. On a mechanical grinder, the handle turns an auger inside a cylinder in the housing. As it turns, the auger forces meat chunks from the hopper toward the knife and plate.

The Knife. The knife, usually with four blades, fits onto the end of the auger shaft and turns as the handle turns the auger. The knife fits flush against the circular plate. When the auger forces meat against the plate and into the holes in the plate, the knife cuts the meat and forces it into the holes.

Mechanical Meat Grinder

Obviously, the knife should be kept sharp. Your sausage supply dealer may sharpen the knives for you, or perhaps refer you to some such service. I sharpen my own with the aid of a large whetstone. The knife is placed flush against the stone and worked in a figure-eight motion. (There may be better sharpening schemes, but I think it's a mistake to start filing on the blade at an angle. Remember that the blade should fit flush against the plate.) When you purchase your grinder, you may want to order an extra blade or two.

The Plate. The plate, round and about ⅛ inch thick, fits into the grinder housing in contact with the cutting edges of the knife. The plate has geometrically spaced holes, through which the sausage meat passes. The size of the holes determines whether the meat is "ground" fine, medium, or coarse. Of course, the smaller holes are more numerous. For most sausages, a plate with 3⁄16-inch holes will be all you need, but it's nice to have other sizes as well.

As a rule, the smaller the diameter of the holes, the more often the plate will have to be cleaned, because stringy tissues clog it up. For this reason, it's sometimes prudent to grind a meat with a ¼- or ⅜-inch plate and then grind it again with a ³⁄₁₆- or ⅛-inch plate. In any case, cutting the meat into small chunks helps reduce the clogging problem. Properly trimming and cutting the meat will take more time, but will save lots of cleaning time during the grinding process.

Before purchasing your grinder, make sure that you can obtain plates of various sizes. The manufacturer may sell these plates directly to users through a customer service department, or they may be available through dealers and mail-order outfits. Each manufacturer of sausage grinders may offer different-size plates, sometimes measured in centimeters. Here's my own classification according to the diameter of the holes:

⅛ inch	=	extra fine
³⁄₁₆ inch	=	medium-fine
¼ inch	=	medium
⅜ inch	=	coarse
½ inch	=	extra coarse

I recommend that the sausage maker have ⅛-, ³⁄₁₆-, and ¼-inch plates. If you are limited to a single plate, go with the ³⁄₁₆ inch. If expense isn't important, get two or three of the ³⁄₁₆-inch plates so that you can change them during the grinding process instead of interrupting the process to clean a plate. (To clean the smaller sizes, by the way, I hold them under running water and poke out the holes one by one with the wooden end of a kitchen match or some such object. Clearly, this is a time-consuming process.)

Be warned that the plate must not turn inside the housing. It is, or should be, held in place by a notch on the perimeter of the plate and a protuberance on the grinder housing. If the plate is not properly installed, the meat tends to mush instead of grind.

Retaining Ring. This large threaded ring fits over the end of the grinder and holds the plate in place. It should be tight, but not tight enough to make the handle difficult to turn.

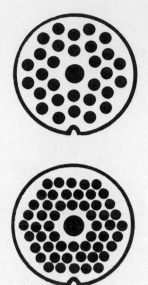

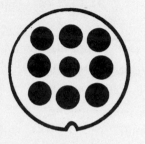

Cutting Plates

Capacity and the Hopper. As a rule, the larger the grinder the larger the auger, knife, and plate, and the more meat the unit will grind per unit of time. The capacity listed by the manufacturer is not without value, but it doesn't really account for cleanup, cleaning clogged plates, and so on. Consequently, the smaller units are just about as good as the larger ones, at least for small sausage-making operations. And, as stated earlier, the smaller units are more likely to be easy to mount.

I would, however, like to see a larger hopper on the smaller units. The idea would be not so much to hold more meat but to keep the meat from falling to the floor. In other words, a wide hopper, within reason, is easier to load.

Sterilization. It's best to sterilize the grinder and all its parts in boiling water before grinding meat. After sterilization, the parts should be chilled before proceeding. Note that harmful bacteria are everywhere.

The trick is not to avoid them entirely, which is impossible, but to minimize their growth. They do not thrive at temperatures below 40 degrees F or above 140 degrees F. Several kinds of potentially harmful bacteria are discussed in Chapter 3 and in the Glossary. The parasitic worm that causes trichinosis is discussed earlier in this chapter.

Electric Grinders

Some people prefer electric meat grinders, and I certainly have no objection to them, provided that they operate with a knife and plate. Most of the electric grinders are freestanding, and therefore don't present mounting problems.

Prices of electric grinders vary, ranging to hundreds of dollars for a commercial unit. Before buying, make sure that you can get extra parts and sausage-stuffing attachments.

Food Processors

I don't recommend food processors and various high-speed zappers for grinding meat because it's difficult to control the consistency and because it's too easy to mush the meat. Some practitioners recommend this type of machine, however, for emulsifying meats for use in frankfurters, bologna, and other such sausages and sandwich meats, making them more like commercial fare. I don't recommend the practice, but suit yourself.

One other consideration is that most food processors don't have sausage-stuffing attachments (discussed in Chapter 3).

Seasonings, Additives, and Spices

All sorts of spices are used in sausage recipes. Some of these give a certain sausage its characteristic flavor, such as the use of fennel in some mild Italian sausages.

Most spices tend to lose flavor and aroma with long storage. It's best to keep them in a dry, cool, dark place. If possible, it's best to purchase or store whole spices, then grind or crush them as needed.

Salt. Historically, salt is the most important seasoning ingredient in a sausage. It still is, especially in sausages that will be hung to smoke or dry for some time, as discussed in Chapter 3. Ordinary table salt will be satisfactory for most sausage making. Sea salt is a little better, at least to me, but it is rather expensive these days.

Black Pepper. Buy whole peppercorns in bulk; then grind or crush your own as needed for making sausage, for cooking, and for table use. To me, the aroma of freshly ground pepper is one of the great small pleasures of cooking and eating.

White Pepper. White pepper is the same as black pepper, only it is harvested earlier. It is not as strong as black pepper.

Paprika. This pepper can be mild (Hungarian paprika) or hot (Spanish paprika). It is used to add color as well as flavor to some sausages.

Red Pepper. Crushed dried chili peppers are often used in sausage making, especially country sausages from the American South, and Spanish or Latin American sausages. Crushed or flaked red pepper, including the hot seeds, is available at most spice markets. Some outlets that specialize in spices market pepper flakes, or whole peppers, in varying degrees of hotness. I prefer to go this route, often selecting a somewhat mild pepper. These milder peppers can be used in recipes in greater bulk, giving more color and flavor without the hotness.

I prefer to buy mild pepper flakes in bulk. For hot red pepper flakes, I usually buy off-the-shelf name brands from my local supermarket, and sometimes I use dried Tabasco peppers from my own garden. Be warned: Wear gloves when seeding hot peppers, and also remove the inner pith as well as the seeds. Do not touch the seeds and pith with your hands and then touch your eyes or tender parts. Pepper burns can be serious.

Additives and Cures. Commercial sausage makers add all manner of extenders and fillers to sausages, such as "corn syrup solids." Some of these are discussed briefly in the glossary, but most of the recipes in this book do not call for such ingredients. Meat is cured primarily by more or less natural salt, some of which may have some of the minerals removed. Sometimes saltpeter, sodium nitrite, and sodium nitrate are mixed in with the salt. A few of the recipes for cured and dried sausages

(Chapter 3) call for such chemicals and cure mixes, but for the most part I omit them.

Spice Mixes for Sausages

Anyone who makes lots of one kind of sausage may want to purchase a spice mix, or, better, might make their own mix. Such a mix can save money and time. Mixes for specific sausages, such as chorizo and bratwurst, are marketed by firms that sell such stuff. See Sources, page 193. My own rather basic mix recipe is set forth below, and it can be modified to suit your taste and fancy.

A. D.'s Basic Sausage Mix

Here's a seasoning for fresh pork sausage that I like to make, using plenty of rather mild red pepper flakes. The mix is enough for 100 pounds of fresh pork. By calculation, the entire batch weighs about 40 ounces, depending on how much pepper you use. To make only 10 pounds of sausage, use 4 ounces of the mix. This amount can be weighed with the aid of a home or office postal scale or a kitchen scale if you have one.

2 pounds regular table salt

2 to 4 ounces ground sage

3 to 4 ounces freshly ground black pepper

1 to 4 ounces red pepper flakes

1 ounce ground coriander

Thoroughly mix all the spices and store in sealed jars. The mix will last for several years, but it's best to use it within a year or so.

Cleanup

Dismantle and wash your sausage mill with soap and hot water as soon as practical after grinding meat or stuffing sausage. Thoroughly dry the knife, plate, and other parts. Store the knife and plate (usually made of carbon steel, which is not stainless) in a plastic bag, and put them into a box along with the rest of the parts.

I use the original packing box for storage. In any case, keep all the parts together. A meat grinder isn't of much use if you can't locate the knife or plate when needed.

During the cleanup and dismantling, you'll find some good sausage meat around the auger inside the housing. While this meat can be taken out at the end of the grinding (and stuffing), I usually leave it in until cleanup time. Then, after washing and storing the sausage mill, I shape the meat into a patty or two, fry it in a skillet, and make myself a sausage patty sandwich with lots of mayonnaise.

For my dog, Nosher, I take this opportunity to fry up any tissue, sinew, and unwanted fat that I trimmed off the meat. That dog loves to make sausages!

Sausage Loaves

Some of the best sausage meats are made in molds or unusual casings. For the most part, the following recipes are quite old and are neglected by modern cookbooks. Consequently, I have given this chapter an old-time theme, except for the last recipe, in which I make use of plastic film and aluminum foil.

One excellent recipe of this sort—haggis—is a specialty of Scotland and is covered in Chapter 8.

Boston Cooking School Sausage

Here's a recipe and stuffing technique from Mrs. D. A. Lincoln's *Boston Cooking School Cook Book*. "Of sweet fresh pork take one third fat and two thirds lean, and chop fine, or have it ground by your butcher. Season highly with salt, pepper, and sage (use whole sage; dry, pound, and sift it). Mix thoroughly. Make cotton bags, one yard long and four inches wide. Dip them in strong salt and water, and dry before filling. Crowd the meat into the bags closely, pressing it with a pestle or potato-masher. Tie the bag tightly and keep in a cool place. When wanted for use, turn the end of the bag back, and cut off the meat in half-inch slices, and cook it in a frying pan until brown. Core and quarter several apples, and fry them in the hot fat and serve with the sausages.

"A safe rule in seasoning sausage meat is one even tablespoonful of salt, one teaspoonful of sifted sage, and a scant half-teaspoon of white pepper to each pound of meat."

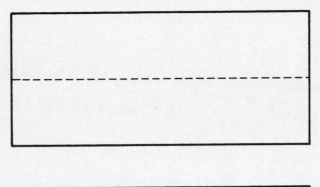

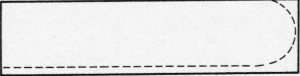

Cloth Casing

Corn Shuck Sausage

Here's an unusual recipe adapted from *The Foxfire Book*. Into 10 pounds of lean pork chunks thoroughly mix ¼ cup salt, ½ cup brown sugar, 2 tablespoons sage, 2 teaspoons black pepper, and 2 teaspoons red pepper flakes. Grind the mixture with a sausage mill. Remove the ears from some corn shucks, pack the sausage inside, tie the end of the shuck closed, and hang in a smokehouse.

The Foxfire Book was short on details, but when I tried this method

I smoked the sausages for 2 hours on one side of a large grill, then put them directly over the coals for a few minutes, turning from time to time. The corn shucks, as many Native Americans knew, added something unique to the flavor. I like to think that this method was suggested to the settlers by Cherokee cookery.

Pennsylvania Ponhaws

Here's an old recipe that I have adapted from *Butchering, Processing, and Preservation of Meat* by Frank G. Ashbrook.

Clean a pig's head, split it, and remove the tongue, eyes, and brains. Put the head halves and tongue into a pot, cover with 4 or 5 quarts of water, bring to a boil, reduce the heat, and simmer for 2 or 3 hours, or until the meat falls from the bones. Turn off the heat, letting the pot cool until the grease rises to the top. Skim off the top. Remove and finely chop the meat. Discard the cleaned bones and strain the stock to remove any bits of gristle or bone. Save out a little of the stock (to be used later) and put the rest back into the pot.

Add the chopped meat. Bring to a new boil and lower the heat to a simmer. Mix a little yellow cornmeal with some of the reserved stock, forming a paste. Mix the paste slowly into the pot, simmering and stirring with a wooden spatula until the mixture thickens almost into a soft mush. Be sure to scrape the bottom as you go to prevent sticking and scorching. Be patient. When the mixture is almost to the mush stage, stir in 1 teaspoon of powdered sage, along with some salt and pepper to taste. Pour the mixture into shallow pans, well greased, and chill as quickly as possible.

When the ponhaws sets, slice and fry until nicely browned. If you prefer, the slices can be dusted with flour before frying. Ponhaws can be refrigerated for several days or frozen for longer storage.

Philadelphia Scrapple Croquettes

I, a hopeless scrapple buff, opened my edition of *Pennsylvania Dutch Cook Book,* a work first published back in 1935, with great expectation. The index listed nine recipes. Going to the first one, I opened to a chapter called "Ways with Philadelphia Scrapple." Interesting stuff—but there wasn't a single recipe for actually making scrapple. Most people, I surmised, purchased it ready-made at the market.

The author of the book also had high praise for Pennsylvania Dutch sausage, but failed to give a single sausage recipe. An essay at the end of the book called "Around the Food Season with my Grandmother at the Farm" did contain some good information:

"With meat grinders, large mixing bowls, and sausage stuffing machines, my grandparents would produce, before my astounded young eyes, a wide variety of foods; fresh pork sausage, smoked beef and beef sausages, Lebanon style bologna, highly spiced, liverwurst, and half a dozen other wursts. These Pennsylvania Dutch women did not flinch at their job of handling freshly killed animals; they had centuries of experience from childhood. They made meat jellies and pigs-feet jelly (a most delightful dish).

"Only in Pennsylvania Dutch territory have I even eaten the fresh pork sausages in the style they made, or the smoked beef sausages. The Lebanon bologna, 5 inches in diameter, is probably over-spiced for most tastes, but it surely is appetizing."

Well . . . my mouth waters as I long for the recipes for the sausages and scrapple. In any case, here's one of the recipes for cooking with scrapple, either made at home or purchased at market.

1 cup minced scrapple

2 hard-boiled chicken eggs, finely chopped

1 chicken egg, whisked

1 cup cooked white rice or mashed potatoes

½ cup cracker or bread crumbs

1 teaspoon minced parsley

cooking oil or fat

salt and pepper, to taste

Mix the minced scrapple, boiled eggs, rice or potatoes, parsley, salt, and pepper. Shape the mixture into croquettes, dip in whisked egg, roll in bread crumbs, and fry in hot oil, turning to brown all sides. Serve hot with horseradish sauce or green fried tomatoes, which is, somewhat surprisingly, another Pennsylvania Dutch specialty.

✎ Easy Scrapple

You don't have to butcher hogs or deal with hog heads, feet, and innards to enjoy scrapple.

10 pounds pork butt

10 cups white stone-ground cornmeal

2 tablespoons salt

1½ tablespoons crushed dried sage

freshly ground black pepper, to taste

salted water

Chop the pork into ½-inch dice. Put it into a pot, cover with salted water, and simmer for 1 hour or so. Drain the meat. Measure broth, adding enough water (if needed) to make 20 cups. Put the 20 cups back into the pot. Mince the meat or run it through your sausage grinder with a ¼-inch plate. Stir the meat, cornmeal, salt, pepper, and sage into the pot. Bring to a boil and cook, stirring as you go with a wooden spoon, for 5 minutes, or until the mixture thickens. Put the mixture into greased loaf pans. Chill. Unmold and cook, refrigerate, or freeze. To cook, slice the scrapple into ½-inch slices, then panfry in a little oil until brown on both sides, turning once. Serve warm for breakfast.

Old-Time Souse and Head Cheese

These two loaf products are similar. Both are made from the head (including the ears and snout) and feet of hogs. Typically, it has chunks of these parts embedded in the loaf. When the loaf is sliced, bits of these parts appear as half moons and other interesting shapes. There are thousands of recipes. The two used below are quoted from the *Boston Cooking School Cook Book,* cited earlier in this chapter. In this work the author said, "Though seldom seen on modern tables, these dishes when carefully prepared are very acceptable to many who have pleasant recollections of them served at 'grandmother's table.'" In more modern times, I remember one of my aunts making souse and, I assure you, the results were more than acceptable!

♪ Souse

"Take the gristly part of the pig's head, but not the fat; also the ears and feet. Remove the hard part from the feet. Scald or singe the hairs, soak in warm water, and scrape thoroughly. Let them remain in salt and water for 10 hours. Scrape, and clean again, and put them a second time in freshly salted water. With proper care they will be perfectly clean. Put them in a kettle and cover with cold water; skim when it begins to boil; set back and let it simmer till the bones slip out easily. Skim out the meat, and remove the hard gristle, bones, and any superfluous fat. When hard, cut in slices, and brown in the oven."

♪ Head Cheese

"Prepare the same as souse, omitting the vinegar and season with sage. Put into a strainer cloth, and press out the fat. Pack it in jars or moulds. Serve cold, or brown slightly in a frying-pan."

My aunt used a similar recipe, but she left the head cheese in the bag and hung it to drip. That is, the bag was hung over a syrup bucket, which caught the fatty liquid that dripped out. From time to time she would twist the bag, helping the process along. After a few days, the head cheese was sliced and eaten as sandwich fare. I liked to cut it into chunks and eat it on crackers. I still like it that way.

Mobile Pan Ham

Here's an old scrapple recipe, quoted from *Gulf City Cook Book*. This work, published back in 1878, was probably the first "committee" fund-raising cookbook put together in the United States, the committee being formed by the Ladies of the St. Francis Street Methodist Episcopal Church, South, Mobile, Alabama.

"Take a hog's head and feet; boil them until the meat falls from the bones; withdraw them from the liquor, which strain and return to the vessel. Chop the meat very fine; season with pepper, salt, spice, onions chopped fine, thyme, sage, and parsley. Add all to the liquor, adding a sufficient quantity of cornmeal to make a stiff mush. Let it boil 10 minutes, stirring all the time. Pour into a deep pan; when cold, cut in thin slices and fry."

"French" Sausage

The *Gulf City Cook Book,* quoted above, also contained a recipe for "French sausage," made up of minced chicken or turkey stuffed in the skin of chicken necks. It's very good, but these days it may be difficult to get up enough skin-on necks. Talk to your butcher, or save up some necks if you raise your own fryers.

"Chop very fine, or pound in a mortar, equal parts of cold fowls, cream, dried bread crumbs, and boiled onions; season them with salt, pepper, and nutmeg to taste; put them into the neck—skins of poultry—tying the ends, and fry them as you would fry sausages."

Ubaldi Jack's Spicy Southern Sausage

I understand that Lee Iacocca, past president of Chrysler Corporation, once took a managerial auto sales job in the South. Figuring that his name wouldn't help his cause in this part of the country, he changed it to Iacocca Lee—with great success. I have used the same trick with this recipe because "Ubaldi's Southern Sausage" simply didn't play. In any case, it's good stuff made with the aid of aluminum foil. I have adapted the recipe from Ubaldi's *Meat Book.*

3 pounds pork shoulder
1 ounce salt
½ cup cold water
¾ teaspoon freshly ground black pepper
¾ teaspoon hot red pepper flakes
½ teaspoon rubbed sage
¼ teaspoon ground allspice
¼ teaspoon ground nutmeg
⅛ teaspoon ground clove
aluminum foil

Cut the meat into chunks and grind it with a ⅜-inch plate. Then grind it again with a ⅛-inch plate. Mix in the water and seasonings. Shape the mix into a long roll and wrap it in aluminum foil. Refrigerate overnight. For breakfast, slice off some ½- to ¾-inch rounds and panfry or broil for about 20 minutes.

Note: I must point out that hog casings, not aluminum foil, were Ubaldi's first choice for stuffing this mix. If you like the recipe but want the real thing, go directly to the next chapter to read all about sausage casings.

Stuffing Sausages

Casings

Sausages are usually stuffed into casings and formed into links of convenient measure. Traditionally, the casings are animal intestines, stripped, turned, and washed. In times past, the casings were prepared during the butchering process and the sausages were stuffed on the spot. If you butcher your own hogs, you might ask your wife to strip and rinse the casings several times while you salt down the hams.

These days, however, the sausage maker usually purchases casings from meat supply houses. These commercial casings are packed in salt and will last for many months in the refrigerator or even longer in the freezer. I purchase mine in 3-pound hanks by mail order. A hank will make about 100 pounds of sausage. To make a small batch of sausage, I merely cut off what I think I'll need. With regular hog casings, 25 feet will be about right for 10 pounds, allowing a foot or two for waste. (Double the length if you are using sheep casings.) Then I refrigerate the rest until needed again. It would be better, perhaps, to separate the casing into 25-foot lengths, then freeze each strip separately in small Ziploc bags. Maybe I'll do it that way one day.

In most of the stuffed sausage recipes in this book, I specify the recommended casing in the list of ingredients. The size of the casing (the diameter when full) can be very important, as it determines the correct cooking and drying times. Adjustments can be made in most cases, but it's best to use the recommended casing if feasible.

Hog Casings. These are by far the most popular casings, partly because pork itself is so popular for making sausages. Prepared hog casings come in several sizes, often defined in millimeters. In round numbers, it takes 25 mm to equal 1 inch. The Sausage Maker catalog (see Sources) lists four sizes: 29 to 32 mm; 32 to 35 mm; 35 to 38 mm; 38 to 42 mm. For most sausages, a 32 to 35 mm will do. After all, most of us don't want to inventory dozens of different casings.

Sheep Casings. These are smaller than hog casings. They are, of course, used for stuffing the smaller-size sausages such as the French chipolata. I understand that goat casings can be used instead of sheep. Who would know? Sheep casings can be purchased in specific sizes, but they average a little less than 1 inch. I like the smaller kind—about ¾ inch—for stuffing finger sausages, but these are difficult to load onto some stuffing tubes.

Beef Casings. These are larger than hog or sheep casings. They are also thicker and tougher, so that drying times for the sausages are longer. When needed in this book for specific recipes for large sausages, beef casings are specified in the list of ingredients. They are subdivided into rounds, middles, and bungs, depending on which part of the intestine is used. The rounds, about 1½ inches in diameter, aren't much larger than hog casings; they are sometimes used for kielbasa and other sausages. Middles are about 2½ inches in diameter; they are used for some bologna and liverwurst sausages. Bungs are about 4 inches in diameter, or larger; they are used in large bologna and cooked salami.

Collagen Casings. These days most of the commercial sausages made in the United States are stuffed into collagen casings. Collagen is a protein material contained in the connective tissue and bones of animals. After processing, the material is made into casings. They are available from the larger suppliers in a variety of kinds and sizes, some made very thin for fresh sausages and some made thicker (and stronger) for sausages that are to be cold-smoked or dried, or both.

Synthetic Casings. A dozen types of synthetic casings can be purchased from sausage and meat supply houses. Some of these are quite specialized, made for a certain kind of sausage. For example, there is a mahogany-colored synthetic casing that is designed for stuffing sausage meat that contains Liquid Smoke; the idea, of course, is to give the color and flavor of smoke without actually smoking the sausage. I prefer the real thing. But suit yourself. If synthetic casings appeal to you (or, perhaps, if natural casings don't), your best bet is to get catalogs from the sausage supply houses or perhaps check with local meat-processing plants.

Some of the synthetic casings are lined with fiber to make them stronger. Others are lined with protein, which in turn causes the casing to adhere to the meat as it shrinks in the drying process.

Clearly, the home sausage maker operating on a budget shouldn't try to buy large quantities of all these natural and synthetic casings. Assortment kits are available, but I think that the beginner should start with a hank of medium hog casings, then add a hank of sheep casings for franks and finger sausages. Others can be added later.

Sausage-Stuffing Devices and Attachments

Meat Grinder Attachments. Most of the hand-cranked sausage mills can be fitted with a sausage tube. This is a slightly conical metal or plastic tube that is flared on the big end, as shown in the drawing on the next page. To use the tube, remove the cutting plate and knife from the sausage mill. Stick the tube through the retaining ring, seat the flared part into the retaining ring, and attach to the sausage mill. Set the knife and plate aside, as they are not normally used in the stuffing operation.

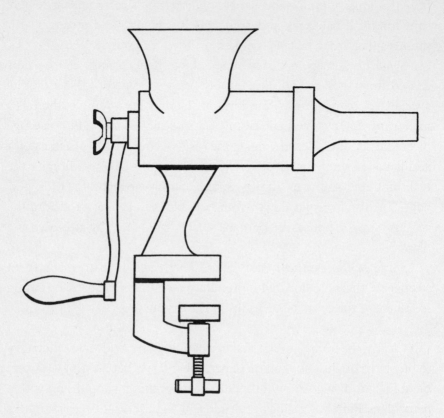

Sausage Tube

Sausage tubes can also be used on many electric meat grinders, but most food processors and other machines that cut meat with a high-speed blade aren't designed for such attachments.

Stuffing Machines. Several stuffing machines are marketed by meat and sausage supply houses. These are nice to have, but they really aren't needed for making small batches of sausage, provided that you have a grinder that works with a stuffing attachment or tube. Available in a number of sizes, the stuffing machines usually work on a screw principle or a lever-operated plunger.

Other Stuffers. Plastic bottles, funnels, and pastry tubes can some-times be modified and used to stuff sausages. It is important that the

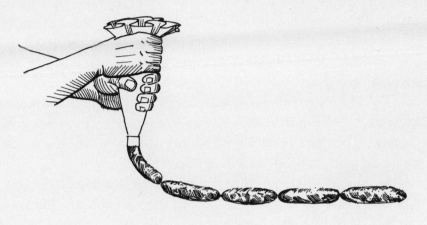

Pastry Tube

tube end fit snugly inside the casing, and that the casing can be gathered onto the tube, accordion-fashion, as discussed below. Sometimes, the home sausage maker will use these makeshift stuffers when the regular attachment is too large for small sheep casings.

Stuffing the Sausage

Regardless of the type of stuffer you use, note that the sausage meat isn't forced through the casing from one end to the other. To force the sausage meat through the casing would either pack the meat much too tightly or burst the skin, or both. When properly gathered onto the tube and fed out, the casing merely slips off the tube as the sausage grows in length. This principle is very important with any sausage-stuffing device, whether it be a $500 commercial machine or a devised handheld tube.

The text below is for a tube attachment used with a hand-cranked meat grinder, which I consider to be by far the more common arrangement. If you use other stuffers, it's easy to modify the procedure as necessary.

Match the Tube and Casing. Many kinds of sausages have an ideal size, or diameter, which means that a certain kind and size of casing should be used for stuffing. But note that a small sheep casing simply won't work properly on a tube designed for medium or large hog casings. The casing will be difficult to thread and feed—and it will probably split at the tube. (Most animal casings are quite strong lengthwise, and in the past have been used for fishing line and other applications. But their strength against bursting is relatively poor.) If your casing doesn't go onto the tube easily, either rig your stuffer with a smaller tube or use a larger casing. All this should, of course, be worked out before you grind the meat. If you have a problem at grinding time, try to keep the sausage meat cold until you work something out.

Get the Casing Ready. If using natural casings, cut them into convenient strips of about 12 feet. Rinse the casings inside and out. The inside can be flushed by running water through the casing, using a hose or faucet. If the casing has been salted for storage, it's best to soak it in cool

Casing Gathered over Tube

36

water overnight, then rinse and flush it. If the casing isn't properly soaked, it may not slip over the tube easily and without splitting.

Loading the Tube. After you have ground all the meat, quickly remove the plate and knife from your sausage mill. Attach the sausage-stuffing tube, tightening it with the threaded retaining ring. Lubricate the tube with a little of the fat from the ground meat. Also, make sure there is a little water inside the casing. Fit one end of the casing over the end of the tube. With your fingers, work most of the casing onto the tube, accordion-style. Leave a few inches loose so that surplus air can escape. The end will be knotted or twisted later.

Other types of stuffer tubes are loaded by the same method. To my way of thinking, the tube is more important than the mechanism, and some expensive machines might well come with tubes that are a little too large.

Stuffing the Casing. After you get the casing gathered onto the tube, load the hopper with ground and ready sausage meat; then turn the crank or otherwise force the meat into the casing. Go slowly. It's best to hold the end of the tube with your left hand, making sure that the casing feeds correctly off the tube, while turning the crank with your right hand. Don't force the meat. Packing the casing too tightly can burst the casing during the stuffing operation, during the linking process, or while cooking. Also, avoid making air pockets in the casing if possible.

Linking. When the length of casing that you threaded onto the tube has been stuffed, inspect the sausage visually for air pockets. Prick the skin of the casing as needed to release the air. Twist the far end of the casing. Then, using both hands, shape a link of suitable size; hold the sausage with both hands and twirl the link, twisting the ends several times. Repeat this process until the entire length has been linked. The exact length of the links isn't too important, although some sausages are traditionally stuffed in standard sizes. You might want to stuff a particular sausage to yield a serving per link.

When the stuffed and linked sausage dries to the touch, the ends will hold together when cut. Usually, the sausages are left joined for hanging or storing. If you don't trust the twisted links to hold, you can

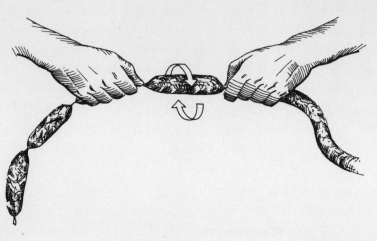

Making Links

always tie the sausage off with cotton string. As a general rule, I twist small sausages but tie larger ones, such as bologna.

Making and Cooking Fresh Sausages

Fresh sausages are not cured and can be cooked right away. They can be kept in the refrigerator for a day or two, which will sometimes help the flavors blend, but for longer storage they should be frozen. Usually, fresh sausages are made with fresh pork and should be cooked thoroughly. The short recipe below, although used mainly as an example, should not be taken lightly! The procedure assumes that you are using a hand-cranked sausage mill that has a suitable stuffing attachment. I have gone into detail on the grinding and stuffing operations that were described above and in Chapter 1. Sometimes a little repetition isn't a bad thing.

10 pounds fatty Boston butt
4 tablespoons salt
2 tablespoons crushed dried sage
2 tablespoons freshly ground black pepper
1 to 2 tablespoons finely crushed red pepper

Soak some medium-to-small hog casings overnight in cold water. Rinse the casings and run some water through them, using a water hose or faucet. Sterilize your sausage mill and its parts in boiling water. Cool and assemble the mill. Cut the meat (partly frozen, if feasible) into chunks suitable for grinding, trimming off sinew and tough tissue. Spread the chunks over your work surface. Mix all the spices and sprinkle them evenly over the meat. Grind with a $\frac{3}{16}$-inch plate.

Quickly remove the sausage knife and plate, placing them in the sink for washing later; don't waste time by washing them now. Quickly install the stuffing tube, securing it with the retaining ring. Carefully start the end of the casing over the end of the tube. Gather the casing around the tube. This should go smoothly. If not, add a little water to the inside of the casing for lubrication. I usually thread on 10 or 12 feet of casing, but the exact amount isn't too important. When you have gathered the casing around the tube, fill the hopper with ground meat and turn the crank, adding more meat to get it coming out the tube. Go slow, helping the tube along with your left hand. Don't stuff the casing too tight, remembering that you'll have to link it later. Stuff all the casing, or a good part of it, then go over it with your hands, smoothing out any lumps. Using a large sterilized needle, prick the skin to eliminate any large air bubbles. Twist the far end of the sausage, then twist it closed. Holding the end with one hand, squeeze into the sausage with your right hand, separating the stuffing. Then, using both hands, sling the link over and over, as when jumping rope, thereby twisting the casing a number of times. When all the sausage has been stuffed into casings and linked, dry the sausage to the touch. At this time, the links can be cut and separated in the twisted part. Usually, it's best to leave two or more links connected.

Now you have a complete fresh sausage. It should be either cooked right away, refrigerated for a day or two, or frozen for longer storage. For frying a fat sausage, most experts agree that the links should be pricked with a fork and simmered in a little water or stock for 15 or 20 minutes. Then they are dried with paper towels and sautéed in a skillet until nicely browned on all sides. I endorse this practice, but I sometimes like to panfry the sausages without the poaching process. Cutting slightly dried sausages in half lengthwise helps them cook through, and I also slice them into wheels before cooking. The diameter of the sausage should also be considered, and the small finger sausages made in sheep casings, as in the next recipe, are much easier to cook.

Note: You can also cold-smoke these sausages for a hour or so before storing or cooking. See the instructions later in this chapter.

Small Breakfast Sausage

For this recipe you'll need sheep casings. The sausage links should be about the size of a finger. These small sausages, or a similar recipe, are often sautéed and served for breakfast, or as a finger food. In either case, an electric skillet will work. They can also be used in kabobs, preferably grilled over charcoal or wood coals, or cooked in soups and stews. Pork butt is specified in the ingredients, but any rather fatty pork will do. The fat content should be about 30 percent, so you can use 7 pounds of lean pork and 3 pounds of pork fat, or thereabouts. Note that the pork will cut and grind easier if it is partly frozen.

10 pounds pork butt

4 tablespoons salt

2 teaspoons freshly ground black pepper

1 teaspoon ground nutmeg

1 teaspoon dried sage

1 teaspoon dried marjoram

4 cups cold water

sheep casings

Cut the pork into chunks suitable for grinding. Spread it out on your work surface. Thoroughly mix the salt and spices, then sprinkle the mix evenly over the pork chunks. Grind the chunks with a ⅛-inch plate, or grind twice with a ³⁄₁₆-inch plate. Using your hands, mix in the cold water. Stuff into sheep casings. These sausages can be cooked immediately, refrigerated for a few days, or frozen for longer storage.

To cook, sauté, broil, or grill the sausages, making sure that the pork is well done, which isn't much of a problem with sausages of small diameter.

Note: You can also cold-smoke these sausages for a hour or so. See the instructions later in this chapter.

Recipes for Cooking Fresh Link Sausages

Links of sausage are often fried in a skillet, broiled, or grilled. They are very good when cooked over charcoal, especially if they contain quite a bit of fat. The fat, of course, keeps the sausage from drying out too much—but it also tends to cause fires in the grill, so that cooking sausage is a full-time job. No recipes are needed for cooking stuffed fresh sausages, but here are a few that I highly recommend. Other recipes are scattered throughout the book.

Shaker Sausage with Apple Rings

The Shakers, perhaps the best American cooks, believed that the Kingdom of God can be achieved right here on earth. This recipe, which I have adapted from the *Heritage Cook Book,* comes pretty close. It can be made in an electric skillet.

The Sausage and Sauce

¾ pound pork sausage
1 cup apple cider
¼ cup chopped onion
1 tablespoon flour
1 tablespoon minced fresh parsley
salt

Heat about ½ inch of water in a skillet. Simmer the sausage for 5 minutes, pricking them with a fork to release some of the fat. Drain the liquid from the skillet. Continue to cook the sausage until they brown, turning several times. Drain off all but 2 tablespoons of the fat that cooked out of the sausage. Set the sausage aside to drain.

Sauté the onion for 5 or 6 minutes. Stir in the flour and a little salt, stirring with a wooden spoon. Add the cider; cook and stir until bubbly. Stir in the parsley. Put the sausage back in the skillet, cover, and heat through. Place the sausage on a heated serving platter. Put the sauce from the skillet into a serving container. Serve the sausage with the sauce and honeyed apple rings.

Honeyed Apple Rings

4 apples
½ cup honey
2 tablespoons vinegar
¼ teaspoon ground cinnamon
salt, to taste

Core but do not peel the apples. Slice them into ½-inch wheels. In a wide saucepan, mix the honey, vinegar, and salt. Bring almost to a boil. Add the apple rings and cook, turning frequently, for about 12 minutes, sprinkling with cinnamon. Serve hot with the sausage and sauce.

Hoppin' John with Sausage

Traditionally eaten on January 1 for good luck during the year, this dish is usually made with dried black-eyed peas, sometimes called cowpeas. It can be made with spicy sausage or with smoked ham hocks, or, better, with both. Some recipes call for cooking the onions with the peas, but I think my way is better in flavor and texture.

1 pound dried black-eyed peas
1 pound pork sausage (hot and spicy)
½ pound smoked ham hocks
2 large, mild white onions, chopped
1 tablespoon red pepper flakes
1 tablespoon lard or cooking oil
salt, to taste
3 or 4 cups cooked long-grain rice (cooked separately)

In a large Dutch oven or other similar pot, cover the peas with about a quart of water and add the ham hocks. Bring to a boil, reduce the heat, cover tightly, and simmer for 2 hours. Add more water if needed. Pull the meat from the ham hock, chop it, and add it back to the pot, along with salt and red pepper flakes. Cut the sausage into ¾- to 1-inch segments. Heat the lard or oil in a skillet and brown the sausage wheels. Pour off the grease and add the sausage to the peas. Simmer for a few minutes while you prepare the rice and chop the onions. You may need to add a little more water at this point; the peas should have some juice. Serve the peas, rice, and chopped onions separately. Spoon a dollop of rice into a bowl, top with peas (making sure everybody gets an equal share of sausage and chopped ham hock), and sprinkle liberally with chopped onions. Serve with corn pone.

Variation: If you have fresh vine-ripened tomatoes, chop two and serve in a bowl to be sprinkled atop the Hoppin' John along with the chopped onions.

✒ Pennsylvania Dutch Fried Sausage

The Pennsylvania Dutch were fond of pork sausages and cooked them in a number of ways. Here's an old favorite.

2 pounds fatty pork sausage links
1 cup bread crumbs
½ cup flour
2 chicken eggs, whisked
salt, to taste
1 tablespoon cooking oil

Mix the eggs, flour, bread crumbs, and salt. Heat the oil in a skillet. Dip the sausages into the egg mixture, then fry them slowly until they are nicely browned and cooked through. Serve these with sauerkraut.

Note: If your sausages contain very little fat, increase the measure of cooking oil.

✐ Sausage in Potatoes

For this recipe, use small pork sausages or franks. These should be fully precooked, preferably by steaming or simmering.

6 small pork sausages or hot dogs

2 cups mashed potatoes

1 large chicken egg (separated)

1½ tablespoons minced green onion with part of green tops

bread crumbs

oil for deep frying

milk

salt, to taste

Mix the mashed potatoes, green onion, 1 egg yolk, and salt. Whisk the egg white along with a little milk. Rig for deep frying. When the oil is hot (about 350 degrees F), coat the sausages with the mashed potato mixture. Roll the logs in bread crumbs, then in the egg white, and again in the bread crumbs. Fry the logs until nicely browned. Serve hot.

Cured-Meat Sausages

When making fully cured or dried sausages, the meat itself must be salt-cured before the casings are stuffed. The meat can be ground and then cured, but I almost always prefer to cure the meat in chunks before grinding it. Of course, the meat can be cured in large pieces, as in hams, but this way requires lots of time for salt penetration and equalization. When cut into 2-inch cubes, the meat can be cured in about 48 hours.

To cure the meat, cut it into chunks of a size suitable for grinding. Spread the meat out in a large plastic tray, sprinkle evenly with salt or a salt cure (according to the recipe you are using), toss to coat all sides, cover, and place in the refrigerator, or in a very cool place, for 48 hours.

As mentioned earlier, the trays work best for 10 pounds of meat if they are long, wide, and shallow. Heavy polyethylene trays made especially for food handling are ideal. These are usually about 25 inches long and 16 inches wide, which fits nicely into my refrigerator after I clean off a whole shelf. Measure, however, before you buy.

Salt is the ingredient that cures meat. There are, it's true, some additives that many people use and believe to be necessary, and several chemicals are used—in very small amounts, as the law allows—in commercially cured meats and meat products. Most of these chemicals give meat a redder color, but how effective they are as curing agents has been questioned and they are believed to cause cancer in animals. But the chemicals are probably harmless if used in moderation, and, in fact, they have been used in meat curing for two thousand years. These cures include sodium nitrite, sodium nitrate, saltpeter (potassium nitrate), ascorbic acid, and others. A few of the recipes in subsequent chapters call for some of these chemicals, and they are also discussed in the Glossary. Because popular and journalistic opinion as well as official guidance tends to change over time, anyone who is concerned about such additives in our meats should get in touch with the consumer affairs offices of the U.S. Department of Agriculture and the Federal Drug Administration, both in Washington.

To use these ingredients, it's always best to measure them carefully and mix them with a small amount of salt, making what is called a cure. The small amount of salt used in the cure is called a carrier; its purpose is to facilitate equal mixing with the meat and other ingredients. The cure is always mixed with lots of regular salt before it is used in the recipe.

There are several commercial cures suitable for making sausage. It is best to follow the manufacturer's instructions unless you have very good reason to deviate. A few cures are described below.

Prague Powder

Prague Powder is a meat-curing trade term for a mixture of sodium nitrite and common salt or of sodium nitrite, sodium nitrate, and common salt. The recipes below are based on formulations set forth by Rytek Kutas in *Great Sausage Recipes and Meat Curing*. The author runs a mail-order house specializing in sausage making, and for some reason or another the terms have been changed to read Insta Cure.

☙ Prague Powder 1 or Insta Cure 1

This mix is not normally used in fresh sausage. It can be used in "cured sausage" that is not fully dried. Recipes for several such sausages are set forth in this book, in which the meat is salted and cured for two or three days before the sausage is stuffed.

1 pound salt

1 ounce sodium nitrite

Thoroughly mix the salt and sodium nitrite. Uneven mixes will result in too much sodium nitrite in some parts of the sausage and not enough in others. For each 10 pounds of meat to be used in the sausage, add 2 teaspoons of Prague Powder 1. Unused Prague Powder 1 can be stored in a dry jar.

Note that the Prague Powder 1 is dissipated after about 2 weeks, making it unsuited (the theory goes) for long cures.

☙ Prague Powder 2 or Insta Cure 2

This cure is intended to be used in sausage that is cured and dried, and can be eaten without cooking. The sodium nitrate in the formula breaks down, over time, into sodium nitrite, thereby giving the cure an extended working life. It is used in sausage that is cured and then dried for several weeks.

1 pound salt

1 ounce sodium nitrite

0.64 ounce sodium nitrate

Thoroughly mix all the ingredients. Add to chunks of meat just before the curing period. (In this book, the meat is cut into chunks, sprinkled with salt, and cured in the refrigerator before grinding.) Use exactly 2 teaspoons for each 10 pounds of meat to be ground. Unused Prague Powder 2 can be stored in a dry jar.

A Saltpeter Cure

Jack Ubaldi, coauthor of *Meat Book*, champions the use of saltpeter in cured meats. The mix can be used for cured hams and other products, and it can be used in many of the recipes in this book simply by substituting the cure for the salt in the recipe. For example, if the recipe calls for 8 tablespoons of salt, simply use 8 tablespoons of the saltpeter cure.

4 pounds salt
1 pound sugar
1¼ ounces saltpeter

Thoroughly mix the salt, sugar, and saltpeter. When properly stored in a jar, the mix will keep for several years.

Other Cures

Morton's salt company and other firms offer cures. These are marketed by mail order, meat outlets, and sometimes large supermarkets. Cumberland General Store (see Sources, page 193) is a good source for the Morton products.

Dried Sausage

A cured and dried sausage is rather firm to the finger and chewy, like hard pepperoni. Often it is thinly sliced before serving, or before using in recipes. Some highly spiced dried sausages, such as dried Spanish chorizo and Chinese sausages, work best in recipes that require steaming or long simmering. Several recipes for making and cooking with dried sausages are set forth in subsequent chapters. Meanwhile, here's a rather basic Italian-style dried sausage, without a long list of flavoring spices or herbs, that I recommend for openers. Note that this recipe has the following ingredients that discourage the growth of bacteria: salt, saltpeter, and wine. Some recipes for dried sausage even have vinegar and brandy, along with red pepper. It is also important to note that the pork is certified (as discussed in Chapter 1), that the meat is kept cold, and that it is hung in a dry place at a cool temperature. Also, don't underestimate the importance of "dry," which clearly implies the absence of moisture, without which bacteria can't thrive.

As a rule, dried sausages may contain a little less fat than a fresh sausage. In the recipe below, try a rather lean Boston butt or similar cut with about 20 percent fat. Measure out 8 pounds lean and 2 pounds fat if you prefer. Both the lean and the fat should be certified. Also, remember that it's best to start off with partly frozen meat; it cuts easier, it grinds better, and it's safer.

10 pounds rather lean pork butt (certified)
1 cup dry red wine
5 cloves garlic, minced
5 tablespoons regular table salt or sea salt
2½ tablespoons freshly ground black pepper
2 teaspoons Prague Powder 2 (optional)
hog casings (medium)

Trim and cut the meat and fat into chunks suitable for grinding. (Be sure to avoid long strings of sinew or tough tissue that can clog up your grinder's plate and knife.) Place the meat into a wide plastic tray (small enough to fit into your refrigerator). Thoroughly mix the salt and Prague Powder. Sprinkle the mix (now called a cure) evenly over the meat chunks, mix thoroughly with clean hands to coat all sides of the meat with the cure, cover, and place in the refrigerator for 48 hours. (If you have a cool place other than the refrigerator, fine. Just remember that it's best to keep the temperature under 50 degrees F.) This will salt-cure the meat.

When you are ready to proceed, sterilize the meat grinder and its parts in boiling water. Cool, assemble the parts, and mount the grinder on a clean work surface. Remove the meat tray from the refrigerator and place the meat on a work surface near the sausage mill. Grind the meat with a ³⁄₁₆-inch plate, feeding it into a tray. (I like to place the ground meat as well as the meat chunks into a double tray unit with crushed ice in the bottom unit. This step isn't necessary if you can grind and stuff the sausages quickly. The point is that it's best to keep the meat cold at all times during cutting, curing, grinding, and stuffing.)

When the meat is ground, sprinkle it evenly with the black pepper, garlic, and wine. Mix thoroughly with your hands. Quickly rig for stuffing by removing the meat grinder's knife and plate, replacing them with a stuffing tube. Quickly thread the washed and rinsed casings over the tube. Stuff the sausages evenly, pricking the casing with a needle as needed to relieve any large air bubbles. When the stuffed casing grows long, twist the end and link every 4 to 6 inches or so. Cut the links in pairs (or perhaps by fours) and hang them to dry in your refrigerator or other cool, dry place. The temperature should be between 34 and 40 degrees F. An airy place is desirable, but too much flow of air can dry the outside of the sausage before the inside ages properly. The humidity in the drying chamber will also have a bearing on how long it takes the sausage to dry, but usually the home sausage maker will have to make do with what he has—and usually the refrigerator is hard to beat. Also, the size of the casing as well as the temperature will have an influence on the drying times.

Hang the sausages for 6 to 8 weeks, or until they are hard to the touch. When properly dried, the sausages are fully cured and can be stored in or out of the refrigerator. I prefer to wrap mine in plastic film or aluminum foil (to prevent further drying) and then keep them in the refrigerator or freezer until needed.

A properly air-dried sausage made from certified pork can be eaten without cooking, but I prefer to cook mine by steaming or using them in soups and stews. A number of recipes for cooking such sausages are set forth in subsequent chapters. See, for example, the excellent recipes for chorizo in the next chapter.

Although thoroughly dried sausages can have a texture and flavor all their own, the main purpose of drying (especially from a historical viewpoint) is to preserve the meat. Often, such sausages are called summer sausage because they are cured in cool weather and last on into summer. There are dozens of such sausages, some of which are described in recipes in subsequent chapters. The recipe above is intended to illustrate how such sausages should be made safely.

Remember also that dried sausages, as well as fresh and semi-dried sausages (covered next), can be smoked for a while to enhance the flavor. But also remember that smoking adds very little to the preservation of the sausage.

Note that the recipe above calls for Prague Powder 2. This ingredient, discussed earlier, contains both sodium nitrite and sodium nitrate, both of which experts think are necessary for making dried sausages. I can take it or leave it in the sausages that I make. If eating another person's sausage, frankly, I would prefer the use of a cure containing both sodium nitrate and sodium nitrite. Suit yourself. Before leaving dried sausage, let's make one without any such cure and without going into quite the detail used above. Then we'll move on to a semi-dried sausage—dried more for flavor than for preservation.

Dried Cervelat or French Summer Sausage

For this recipe, we'll use a combination of lean beef, lean pork, and pork fat, along with white wine. You can also use veal instead of beef. It's best to start with partly frozen meats and fat.

4 pounds lean beef

4 pounds lean pork (certified)

2 pounds fresh pork fat (certified)

2 cups dry white wine

1 large onion, grated

10 cloves garlic, minced

6 tablespoons salt

3 tablespoons freshly ground black pepper

hog casings

Cut the meats and fat into chunks suitable for grinding. Mix the meats in a plastic tray, sprinkle evenly with salt, cover, and refrigerate for 48 hours. Grind the meats with a ³⁄₁₆-inch plate. With your hands, mix in the black pepper, garlic, onion, and wine. Stuff the mix into medium hog casings, link every 4 to 6 inches, and hang to dry for 4 weeks.

At the end of the 4-week period, mix the following in a small saucepan:

¼ cup dry white wine

½ teaspoon dried thyme

½ teaspoon dried sage

2 bay leaves, crushed

Bring the mixture to a boil and let cool. Rub or brush the sausages with the mixture, then hang them to dry for another 4 weeks, or until hard to the touch.

Semi-Dried Sausages

A few recipes call for partly drying a sausage, which, of course, produces a texture somewhere between soft fresh sausages and hard, dried cured sausages. Sometimes, hanging the sausage for a certain period of time ages it, allowing its flavors to develop, as in Lebanon bologna in Chapter 14.

Some of the sausages that are usually dried, such as pepperoni, can be semi-dried, giving a different texture suitable for topping pizza. How dry should it be? That's up to you. Just remember that a semi-dried sausage should be treated as though it were fresh. I have eaten sausages, fully cooked in such recipes as stews, at all stages of the drying process. This allows me to eat some of the sausage without having to wait eight weeks, and it gives me experience with what happens during the drying process.

Semi-dried sausages can be wrapped and frozen.

Cold-Smoking Sausages

Cold-smoking can be a part of the curing process, usually done at the start of the drying time. But remember that smoke does very little to preserve the meat. Salt-curing and drying are the operative principles in curing meats and sausages suitable for long storage without refrigeration. Smoke does, however, add considerably to the flavor and color of meats and fish, and it can work wonders on pork sausages. Hot-smoking, as discussed below, merely adds some smoke while cooking the sausage. Cold-smoking at temperatures below 100 degrees F—preferably below 70 degrees F—does not cook the sausage and permits it to be smoked for relatively long periods of time.

Often, cold-smoking works with dry-curing sausage, in which case several hours or a day or so in a cold-smoker can be considered the first part of the overall drying time of four to eight weeks or longer, depending on the size of the sausage and the kind of casing.

I have treated smokehouses and the cold-smoking process at some length in my book *Cold-Smoking & Salt-Curing Meat, Fish, & Game,* and I can't rewrite the book here. In essence, however, all you need for cold-smoking is a smoke chamber and a smoke generator. The smoke generator, of course, requires heat, either from wood, charcoal, gas, or electricity. You don't want too much heat in the smoke chamber if you are trying to cold-smoke. Consequently, the smoke generator is often removed to some distance from the chamber, allowing the smoke to cool down. Obviously, the ambient temperature is very important for cold-smoking operations. It's difficult, for example, to cold-smoke when the outside temperature is 102 degrees F. Normally, cold-smoking in most parts of the United States is easier to accomplish during the winter months.

The kind of wood used to make smoke isn't as important as people think, especially with highly seasoned sausages. I recommend using any good hardwood, either in chips, chunks, or sawdust. Further, I prefer freshly cut green wood to dry wood that has to be soaked in water.

If you smoke a lot of sausages, you might consider buying a commercial smoker with thermostats and other controls. The small electric smokers will do a good job (without using the water pan) if the temperature can be kept low enough. You can also build a walk-in smokehouse or rig some sort of barrel or box smoker with the heat source placed some distance away.

The key to any cold-smoking operation, of course, is the temperature inside the smoke chamber. A thermometer inside the chamber is the best guide to exactly what's going on. Once you have the smoke coming at the right temperature, it's really easy to smoke link sausages. They are simply hung vertically from rods or hooks. Large sausages such as bologna are hung by the end, sometimes with the aid of a string, but smaller link sausages are usually hung in pairs.

After cold-smoking for a day or so (sometimes depending partly on the recipe), the sausages are then hung in a cool place—34 to 40 degrees F—to dry or semi-dry, as discussed above and in some of the recipes in the subsequent chapters.

Of course, fresh sausages can be cold-smoked for a few hours for flavor, then cooked, refrigerated, or frozen. These are not cured and should therefore be thoroughly cooked, refrigerated, or frozen.

Hot-Smoked Sausages

Most fresh sausages can be cooked on a grill heated by charcoal, wood, gas, or electricity. Add some wood chips and you've got hot-smoked sausages. Some recipes, such as the Boerish sausage in Chapter 12, work especially well on a grill, but the truth is that most fresh sausages can be hot-smoked successfully.

I like sausages cooked directly over the heat, but the indirect method in a closed-hood grill will produce more smoke. That is, the heat is on one side of the grill and the sausages on the other. Wood chips are placed on or around the heat source, producing a dense smoke under the covered hood. To cook the sausages, the temperature under the hood should be at about 200 degrees F. The lower the temperature, the longer the cooking time and the stronger the smoke flavor. The complete outdoor chef, of course, will be adept at controlling the temperature with the amount of fuel and the air flow (oxygen). One good method is to smoke the sausages by the indirect method, then finish them off directly over the coals. Direct and indirect grilling can be accomplished best with large covered grills, whether the style be rectangular, kettle, or barrel.

For flavor, I think that freshly cut green wood is really better, and a good deal cheaper, than dry wood purchased in bags. Hickory, apple, pecan, oak, and so on will be just fine.

Those people who have a cooker/smoker can also cook sausages to perfection. Typically, these units have a heating element (or charcoal pan) in the bottom, on which the wood chips are piled. Over the heating element is a water pan, which provides moisture and helps keep the temperature low owing to the latent heat of evaporation. I question whether using the water pan is always a good idea, but suit yourself and follow the manufacturer's instructions. Just make sure that you are *cooking* the sausages. Some "smokers" with electric heat may not get hot enough to cook the sausage when used in cold, windy weather—but they may get too hot for cold-smoking. If in doubt, rig a thermometer inside the smoker and check the temperature from time to time. It should be at least 150 degrees F in order to cook the sausage, and 200 degrees F will work better. Some of these cookers come with a temperature indicator, but they are not very reliable and often reflect low, medium, or hot, instead of degrees Fahrenheit.

I like to cook sausages on a grill directly over wood coals, with a few wood chunks along the edge. Wood coals produce more smoke and are hotter than charcoal. Cooking over wood is a full-time job. This is especially true with pork sausage because the fat drips out, causing lots of smoke and sometimes fires. I like hot-smoked sausages prepared on a large grill, along with steaks, chops, and other meats or even fish, and perhaps some quartered pineapples. Typically, sausages grilled and hot-smoked by this method will be quite done on the outside, browning and crisping the casing, but juicy and tasty on the inside, bursting and squirting flavor when you bite into one. It's a gustatory experience like no other.

4

Iberian and Latin American Sausages

Spain, for the most part, has a much warmer climate than the rest of Europe. As a result, foods tend to go bad quicker, and sausage is no exception. To help keep the meat palatable and safe to eat before the days of mechanical refrigeration, more spices were used, along with such preservatives as salt and vinegar and booze.

Although both Spain and Portugal have a number of regional sausages, it is the highly spiced ones that have dominated the cuisine in the homelands as well as in Mexico and other Spanish and Portuguese parts of the New World.

Fresh Chorizo

This classic Spanish sausage, also popular in Latin America, is distinguished by chili peppers, vinegar, and spices. For best results (in my opinion), use a lot of rather mild red peppers, well seeded, so that you get the flavor and color without all the heat. Since there is a good deal of difference between one pepper and another, experience is the best guide. If in doubt, fry a small patty and taste it before stuffing the whole batch into casings. Then you can add more meat if the mix is too hot. If it's not hot enough, mix in some cayenne. For the pork, I usually use fresh pork butts or shoulders that are about 25 percent fat. If in doubt, weigh the lean and fat separately, then use 6 pounds lean and 2 pounds fat. Of course, other cuts of pork can also be used, and the fat can be fat-back.

10 pounds fresh pork butt or shoulder
1 ounce dried chili peppers
½ cup red wine vinegar
2 cups water
5 cloves garlic, minced
4 tablespoons salt
2 tablespoons Spanish (hot) paprika
cayenne, to taste (optional)
hog casings

Cut the peppers in half lengthwise, then remove the seeds and membrane. I use a spoon for this. After handling the chili peppers, be sure to wash your hands before you rub your eyes or touch sensitive parts of your body; some people wear rubber gloves when seeding peppers. Bring 2 cups of water to a boil, add the seeded peppers, turn off the heat, and soak for an hour or two. Place the peppers into a food processor, along with the wine vinegar, garlic, salt, and paprika. Puree and hold.

Cut the meat into small chunks and grind with a rather coarse plate, say ¼ inch. Thoroughly mix the puree into the meat. Let stand for 1 hour or so, then take out a little bulk sausage to fry a few patties, if you want to enjoy some of your chorizo immediately. After tasting a patty, add the cayenne if you wish. Stuff the rest in hog casings. Hang in a cool, airy spot and dry for about 2 days. Cook, refrigerate for a few days, or freeze.

These sausages are best when simmered for a long while in such dishes as garbanzo bean soup or paella, covered later in this chapter.

Dried Chorizo

In the past, chorizo has been dried for long storage without refrigeration. In many recipes, saltpeter or sodium nitrite or some such cure is used, but ordinary salt will do if you use enough of it. (If you want to use a cure, however, see the instructions in Chapter 3.) When drying the sausage, it helps to have a cool, airy, and dry atmosphere. If you live in a mountain climate that stays at a relatively constant temperature—between 34 and 40 degrees F—great. If not, you've got a problem. I normally use a section of my refrigerator, as discussed in Chapter 3.

10 pounds fresh pork butt or shoulder (certified)
20 cloves garlic, minced
1 cup salt
½ cup Hungarian paprika
2 tablespoons freshly ground black pepper
1 to 2 tablespoons red pepper flakes
1 tablespoon cayenne
1 cup red wine vinegar
1 cup brandy
2 teaspoons crushed fennel seed
2 teaspoons crushed cumin seed
2 teaspoons dried oregano
hog casings

Cut the pork into chunks suitable for grinding. Put the chunks into a plastic tray, sprinkle with the salt, coating all sides, cover, and refrigerate for 2 days. When you are ready to proceed, thoroughly mix the dry seasonings into the salty meat. Grind with a ³⁄₁₆-inch plate. Mix in the garlic, wine vinegar, and brandy. Stuff into hog casings, tying off in 4-inch links. Hang in a cool place (34 to 40 degrees F) for 8 to 10 weeks. These sausages, if properly processed, will be thoroughly cured and can be hung without refrigeration. I like to wrap mine in plastic film, however, and refrigerate or freeze them.

Being hard and dried, these sausages are best when used in soups and stews so that they will be simmered for a long time. The flavor is on the strong side, but they are usually used in small quantities.

Mexican Chorizo

Most recipes for chorizo call for hog fat, which, along with beef fat, or suet, is held to be a toxic substance in some quarters. Here's a modern recipe that calls for vegetable shortening. Although pork remains in the ingredients, note that lean pork does not contain fat marbled in the meat. The use of brandy in a Mexican recipe might raise some French eyebrows, but, according to my source for this recipe (George C. Booth's *The Food and Drink of Mexico*), good brandy has been in production south of the border for 450 years.

2 pounds lean pork
½ cup vegetable shortening
1 pint red wine vinegar
½ cup 100-proof brandy
2 bell peppers, grated
8 cloves garlic, grated
6 bay leaves, crushed
4 tablespoons salt
3 tablespoons chili powder
2 tablespoons Spanish (hot) paprika
1 teaspoon fresh coarsely ground black pepper
1 teaspoon dried oregano
1 teaspoon ground cumin
1 teaspoon dried thyme
½ teaspoon ground cinnamon
½ teaspoon ground clove
¼ teaspoon powdered ginger
¼ teaspoon grated nutmeg
¼ teaspoon ground coriander seed
hog casings

Cut the meat into small chunks and spread it over your work surface. Mix all the herb and spice ingredients, then sprinkle them evenly over the meat along with the grated bell peppers and garlic. Grind the mixture, using a ⅛- or 3⁄16-inch plate. Put the ground meat into a nonmetallic container; mix in the wine vinegar, brandy, and vegetable shortening; cover; and refrigerate for 24 hours. Stuff the mixture into medium hog casings, tie into 4-inch links, and hang in a cool, breezy place for 24 hours. Use immediately, refrigerate for several days, or freeze.

Note: Increase the measures if you want more chorizo.

Cooking with Chorizo

For a long time, chorizo has been a major ingredient in soups and stews. In fact, it may have taken some of the luck out of pot dishes. In the time of the Crusades, the Christians in Spain used chorizo—a pork product—to distinguish themselves from the Arabs. Hence, it became customary to use a little chorizo in just about every pot, in case unexpected company came by.

The tradition was continued in Spanish and Portuguese lands of the New World, where chorizo has become a part of several of what can only be described as national stews. Many of these are quite elaborate, calling for ten or twelve kinds of meats, variety meats (such as pig tails, ears, and snouts), birds, and, almost always, chorizo. The Spanish bean soup, below, is a sample of this sort of stew.

Garbanzo Bean Soup

This filling soup is popular in the Tampa Bay area of Florida, where Cubans provided the labor for the cigar industry years ago. It's very, very good. To cook it, you'll need a large pot—preferably a cast-iron stovetop Dutch oven. The beans are called garbanzo beans, Spanish beans, and chickpeas. They are available by mail order, in specialty foods stores, and often these days in the bean section of large supermarkets. By whatever name, they give a nice and quite surprising crunch to soups. Some people soak the beans overnight in water, perhaps with a little baking soda added, but I prefer to cook them right out of the package.

1 pound chorizo sausage, sliced

2 pounds smoked ham hocks

4 pig's feet, split

1 pound dried garbanzo beans

4 large onions, chopped

8 cloves garlic, chopped

4 medium potatoes, diced

½ green bell pepper, chopped

½ red bell pepper, chopped

1 small cabbage, shredded

salt and freshly ground black pepper, to taste

3 bay leaves

½ teaspoon saffron

water

Put the pig's feet, ham hocks, chorizo, and garbanzo beans into the pot, along with the bay leaves. Cover with water, bring to a boil, reduce the heat, and simmer for 1½ hours, or until tender, adding more water (boiling hot) from time to time if needed. Add the potatoes, onions, garlic, bell peppers, cabbage, saffron, salt, and pepper. Increase the heat until the soup boils, then lower the heat, cover, and simmer until the potatoes are done. Water may be needed all along, but remember that the soup should be quite thick. Serve hot along with plenty of crusty Cuban bread. I sometimes make a whole meal of this soup.

♪ Paella

More and more we see colorful seafood variations of this traditional Spanish dish. The essential ingredients, however, are chicken, rice, and chorizo. Although pimiento strips are traditionally used, they are mostly for garnish; I usually use strips of red bell pepper cooked in the dish. It is best cooked in a special paella pan or a large jambalaya skillet about 13 inches in diameter. A large electric skillet will also work nicely. Part of the pleasure of this dish is in seeing the whole thing. So, serve the dish at the table right out of the skillet or paella pan, letting each diner help himself.

Fish is an excellent addition to a paella, provided that it is fresh and firm so that it holds its shape during cooking and serving. I like to use saltwater sheepshead, which is often used as a substitute for crab meat.

If readily available, I like to use stone crab claws, but other crab claws will work. Squid, eels, scallops, and other seafood can also be used.

The saffron used in the recipe is an expensive Mediterranean ingredient that adds color to the dish. Omit it if you are on a tight budget, or perhaps substitute the colorful annatto oil—an unsung ingredient that gives a nice color—if you have it on hand from culinary adventures in tropical American cooking.

1 pound chorizo, cut into ½-inch wheels
1 fryer chicken, cut into serving pieces
1 pound medium shrimp (whole)
1 pound stone crab claws, cracked
½ pound firm fish fillets, cut into 1-inch chunks
2 dozen shucked oysters, medium size
1 dozen fresh mussels
3 cups uncooked white rice
2 cups chopped fresh tomato
1½ cups chopped onion
10 cloves garlic, minced
½ green bell pepper, cut into thin strips
½ red bell pepper, cut into thin strips
¾ cup olive oil
salt and freshly ground black pepper, to taste
½ teaspoon Spanish (hot) paprika
½ teaspoon ground saffron
boiling water

Wash, trim, and steam the mussels. (Discard any that do not open.) Set the mussels in a pan or dish nested over hot water. Heat the olive oil in a skillet on medium-high heat. Fry the chicken pieces, turning from time to time, until they are lightly browned. Add the chorizo slices. Cook for another 3 or 4 minutes or so, stirring with a wooden spoon. Place the chicken and chorizo on a brown paper bag. Sauté the onion in the remaining oil, stirring as you go, for 5 minutes. Add the tomatoes and turn the heat to high, cooking until much of the liquid has left the tomatoes. Add the red pepper, green pepper, garlic, salt, black pepper, and paprika. Cook for a few minutes, until the pepper is tender. Add the rice and cook for 5 minutes, stirring constantly, until it starts to turn brown. Put the chicken and chorizo pieces back into the pan. Add 4 cups of boiling water. Mix the saffron into a little boiling water, add it to the pan, and mix well.

When the liquid starts to boil nicely, add the stone crab claws. Stir in 3 more cups of boiling water. Cook for 3 or 4 minutes, then add the shrimp and fish chunks. Cook for 3 or 4 minutes, then add the oysters. Cook for another 3 or 4 minutes, or until the oysters start to curl around the edges. Fish out some of the red bell pepper strips. Garnish with steamed mussels and red pepper strips. Place the paella pan on trivets in the middle of the table. Serve hot, spooning the paella directly onto preheated plates, along with plenty of crusty hot bread.

Note that the shrimp in my recipe are not beheaded or peeled, partly because the "fat" in the head adds to the flavor. The peeling is done at the table, using the fingers. If you are serving squeamish folks, however, it will be best to behead, peel, and de-vein the shrimp before adding them to the pot.

Chorizo and Barley

For this Andalusian dish I owe thanks to Bert Greene, author of *Grains Cookbook,* who said he got it while on a tourist excursion out from Madrid. The dish has truly wonderful flavor.

½ to ¾ pound chorizo, cut into wheels

1 cup pearl barley

3 cups chicken stock or broth

½ cup sliced green olives

1 tablespoon butter

1 medium-to-large onion, chopped

¼ teaspoon chopped fresh thyme

chopped fresh parsley, to taste

salt and freshly ground black pepper, to taste

In a saucepan or skillet over medium-low heat, sauté the chorizo until they are browned. (If they are fatty, no grease will be required.) Remove the sausages to drain. Add the butter and sauté the onion for a few minutes. Add the barley and thyme, tossing well. Add the chicken stock and browned chorizo. Bring to a boil, reduce the heat, and simmer for 30 to 40 minutes, or until the barley has absorbed all the liquor. The barley should be tender at this point. If it is too chewy, add a little more broth or water, cooking again until the liquid has been absorbed. If it is too wet, cook uncovered until the liquid had been absorbed. Stir in the olives, along with some salt and pepper to taste. Sprinkle with chopped parsley. Serve hot.

✐ Menudo

Tripe is popular in Mexico and is often cooked with the aid of chorizo, as in this recipe. If you can't find tripe in your meat market, talk to your butcher. I use whole chopped tomatoes in my menudo, but more persnickety cooks may choose to peel and seed them.

2 pounds tripe
1 pound chorizo link sausage
3 tomatoes, chopped
1 medium-to-large onion, chopped
2 cloves garlic, minced
1 tablespoon chopped fresh cilantro
1 teaspoon chopped fresh thyme
1 teaspoon chopped fresh oregano
salt and pepper, to taste
lard or cooking oil

Put the tripe in a pot, cover with salted water (2 tablespoons salt per quart), bring to a boil, cover, reduce the heat, and simmer for 3 hours, or until the tripe is tender. Drain the tripe and cut it into cubes from 1 to 2 inches in size. Heat a little lard or oil in a skillet and sauté the sausage for about 20 minutes. Remove and drain the sausage, then sauté the onion and garlic for 5 or 6 minutes. Remove and drain the onion and garlic. Add more oil to the skillet if needed, then fry the tripe, turning, until it starts to brown.

Put all the ingredients into a stove-top Dutch oven, adding enough water to cover everything. Bring to a boil, reduce the heat, and simmer until the liquid thickens. Serve hot. Feeds 6.

✐ Mexican Meat Loaf

This wonderful dish may be of Arabic origin, going back to the time of the Moors. The Spanish name is *albondigón*, but this version has a Mexican spin.

1 pound chorizo
1 pound ground lean pork
1 chicken breast (both sides)
2 medium-to-large onions
4 chicken eggs
2 cups vinegar
1 cup pitted black olives, chopped
½ cup stone-ground white cornmeal
¼ cup finely chopped cilantro
3 pickled green peppers, minced
2 tablespoons chili powder
2 bay leaves
salt and pepper, to taste

Skin the chicken breast and chorizo. Cut the pork, chicken breast, chorizo, and onions into chunks suitable for feeding into a sausage mill. Mix the chunks, spread them out, and sprinkle evenly with the cornmeal, salt, pepper, and chili powder. Grind the mix with a ³⁄₁₆- or ¼-inch plate. With your hands mix in the chicken eggs, minced peppers, cilantro, and olives. Shape the mixture into a 10-inch loaf. Roll the loaf in a piece of cheesecloth, twisting the ends to make handles. Heat some water in a pot or pan large enough to hold the loaf comfortably; there should be enough water to barely cover the loaf. Add 2 cups vinegar and the bay leaves. When the liquid boils vigorously, place the loaf in the pan. Simmer on low heat for 2 hours. Unwrap the loaf, slice, and serve hot with sliced tomatoes, sliced jícama, sliced avocado, salsa, and refried beans. A drop or two of lemon juice goes nicely on the jícama and avocado.

♪ Chorizo and Lentils

Here's a South American dish that is often cooked with very fatty sausages. If your chorizo are on the lean side, you'll need to add a little cooking oil or hog fat. If you have a choice, use fresh chorizo instead of dried.

1 pound chorizo

1 cup cooked lentils

2 medium tomatoes, peeled and quartered

1 medium-to-large onion, sliced

1 green bell pepper, seeded and sliced

1 fresh hot chili pepper, seeded and minced

2 cloves garlic, minced

salt and pepper, to taste

Cut the chorizo into short lengths and fry in a cast-iron skillet. Drain the chorizo and pour off all but about 2 tablespoons of the grease that cooked out of the sausages. If necessary, add a little oil. Heat the grease, then sauté the lentils, onion, peppers, and garlic for about 10 minutes, stirring with a wooden spoon. Add the tomatoes, browned chorizo, salt, and pepper. Cover and simmer for 10 or 15 minutes. Serve hot.

Linguica (hot smoked)

Also known as longanzia, this Portuguese sausage is made with a dice of pork lean and fat. That's right. No grinding. It is, however, permissible to grind the fat and lean separately with a ¼- to ½-inch plate. Either way, be sure to try this one. Exact measures aren't necessary, but use 10 pounds total, mixed approximately 6 pounds lean to 4 fat.

6 to 7 pounds lean pork

3 to 4 pounds fat pork

10 cloves garlic, minced

10 dried red chili peppers, crushed (or to taste)

3 tablespoons salt

3 tablespoons Spanish (hot) paprika

1 tablespoon freshly ground black pepper

1 tablespoon finely chopped fresh marjoram

¾ cup ice water

½ cup cold cider vinegar or wine vinegar

hog casings

Cut the fat and meats into a dice of ¼ to ½ inch. Thoroughly mix all the ingredients and place them into a plastic tray or other suitable container. Cover and refrigerate for 2 hours. Stuff the mixture into hog casings, tying off into 12-inch links. Hang the links in a cool, breezy place until dry. Cold-smoke at 100 degrees F or less for several hours, then hot-smoke (perhaps on a grill) until the sausage is cooked through and safe to eat. (If in doubt, use a meat thermometer inserted into the center of the sausage; it should read 150 degrees F or better.) If you are not going to cook all the sausage right away, freeze it immediately after cold-smoking, then thoroughly cook it before eating. It can be cooked by poaching, grilling, or broiling.

✎ Mushrooms Stuffed with Linguica

When you make your linguica (or chorizo), save ½ pound of bulk sausage for this recipe. If you are working with stuffed sausage, remove the casing and crumble the mixture.

2 pounds large mushrooms

½ pound bulk linguica (or chorizo)

1 cup chicken stock

1 medium-to-large onion, finely chopped

½ cup soft bread crumbs

2 tablespoons chopped dark raisins

2 tablespoons olive oil

1½ tablespoons minced fresh cilantro

1 teaspoon minced fresh oregano

salt and pepper, to taste

Remove and chop the stems from the mushrooms. Heat the olive oil in a small skillet. Sauté the onion and mushroom stems for about 10 minutes. Mix the onion and mushroom caps in a bowl along with the bread crumbs, sausage, raisins, cilantro, oregano, salt, and pepper.

Preheat the broiler. Arrange the mushroom caps on a baking sheet with the stuffing up. Broil close to the heat for about 5 minutes, or until the tops are golden. Using tongs, arrange the mushrooms stuffing-side-up in a large skillet. (An electric skillet is ideal.) Pour the chicken stock around the mushrooms. Bring the stock to a boil, reduce the heat, cover, and simmer for 15 to 20 minutes. Place the mushrooms on a heated serving platter. Increase the heat to the skillet. Boil the stock until the volume is reduced by half, making a sauce. Pour the sauce over the mushrooms. Serve warm.

Boudin Barbados

The Caribbean area has several blood sausages. This unusual variation from Barbados (as adapted from *The Complete Book of Caribbean Cooking* by Elisabeth Lambert Ortiz) is made with sweet potatoes and pumpkin with a pig's-blood binding. The pumpkin is a West Indian sort called calabaza. Hubbard squash can be substituted. Any fresh chili pepper can be used, but vary the amount according to the heat. Be warned that a full tablespoon of minced bird peppers or habañeros will be hot indeed!

3 pounds sweet potatoes

2 pounds calabaza

1 to 2 cups pig's blood

1 cup finely chopped shallots

1 tablespoon minced fresh thyme

1 tablespoon minced fresh marjoram

1 tablespoon minced fresh hot chili pepper (seeded)

1 teaspoon ground clove

salt, to taste

hog casings

Peel the sweet potatoes and pumpkin. Either grate them or chop and run through a food mill. Mix in the chopped shallots, thyme, marjoram, chili pepper, clove, and salt. Add the pig's blood, a little at a time, until the pudding has a soft consistency. Stuff the mix into medium hog casings, tying into 6-inch lengths.

Place a trivet in the bottom of a large pot, heat some salted water to a boil, add the sausage, and simmer for 20 minutes, or until no juice runs out when the lengths are pricked with a fork. Drain the lengths. Serve hot or refrigerate and reheat as needed.

According to Mrs. Ortiz, these blood sausages are served along with souse (Chapter 2) for a Saturday night meal. They are also served for lunch and as appetizers.

Annatto Sausage

To the European sausage-making traditions, America has contributed red peppers, potatoes, and allspice. Other spices were also used in the New World, and still are. Annatto seeds, for example, add flavor as well as color to various dishes of the Yucatán, Cuba, and the other islands of the Caribbean. The seeds, as well as annatto oil, can be purchased in some ethnic stores or by mail order. The list below calls for ten red peppers. Be careful, however, that you have peppers of medium strength. If you used ten bird peppers from the islands or habañeros from the Yucatán, they might eat up your sausage mill.

10 pounds pork shoulder

¼ cup salt

1 cup annatto seed, crushed

10 dried red peppers, crushed

1 tablespoon ground allspice

1 tablespoon crushed cumin

20 cloves garlic, minced

4 cups cold water

Cut the meat into chunks suitable for grinding. Spread the meat out on your work surface, then sprinkle with the spices and garlic. Grind the meat, mix with the water, and stuff into hog casings. Poach these in hot water for 20 minutes, then dry and grill over charcoal or, better, wood coals. Serve these with grilled fresh pineapple, another Central American product.

Note that a truly American sausage of this sort would not contain pork, which was introduced to the New World by the Europeans. But also remember that the Natives enjoyed fatty meats similar to pork, such as the guinea pig, opossum, armadillo, manatee, and peccary.

Cajun and Creole American Sausages

If cooking is almost a religion in the lower half of Louisiana, my personal Old Testament is the second edition of *The Picayune Creole Cook Book,* first printed in 1901 and reprinted in an unabridged edition in 1971 by Dover Publications. (*The Picayune,* of course, refers to the famous New Orleans daily newspaper.) To this work I stand head over heels in debt not only for the recipes and techniques in this chapter but also for some of the terminology. The *Picayune* recipes were intended for use by the housewife, who, the book says, "generally prepares a sufficient quantity to last several days." Although I have tried to stick to the old-time recipes as much as possible, I take the liberty of using a mechanical sausage grinder instead of "hashing" the meat with a knife.

Andouilles and Andouillettes

This popular Cajun sausage is made with the aid of chitterlings, a word that might not be recognized at first glance by the most enthusiastic andouille fan, who will know them as chitlins. These are the largest intestines of the hog—turned, washed, soaked in water, washed again, and cut into pieces. I can purchase them frozen in my supermarket, and they are available at most meat shops, although they might not be on display. I normally buy them frozen in 10-pound boxes. What I don't use in the andouilles are boiled (outside the house, my wife says) until tender. Then they are dusted with seasoned flour and deep-fried, or boiled and then frozen in small packages for frying at a later date. In any case, this is an excellent sausage. Be sure to try it.

4 pounds lean pork, partly frozen
4 pounds fat pork, partly frozen
2 pounds chitterlings, partly frozen
4 large onions, chopped
10 cloves garlic, chopped
2 tablespoons minced fresh parsley
1 tablespoon minced fresh thyme
1 tablespoon minced fresh sweet marjoram
2 tablespoons salt
2 tablespoons freshly ground black pepper
1 to 2 teaspoons cayenne
1 teaspoon ground mace
1 teaspoon ground clove
1 teaspoon ground allspice
1 teaspoon ground or finely crushed bay leaf
hog casings

Chop the pork, fat pork, and chitterlings into chunks, then mix and spread them out on a work surface. Mix the onions, garlic, parsley, thyme, and marjoram; spread the mixture evenly over the meat. Mix all the remaining dry ingredients and sprinkle evenly over the meat. Grind the mixture in a sausage mill, using a ³⁄₁₆-inch wheel.

If you want andouilles, stuff the mixture into large hog casings. If you want andouillettes, stuff into small hog casings or perhaps sheep or goat casings. Try some of both.

Often, these sausages are simmered in a broth or poached in milk, then broiled, grilled, or baked. When freshly made, they will keep for a few days in the refrigerator, or they can be frozen. Also, they can be poached and then frozen.

Andouilles are often served with mashed potatoes. Try them grilled and served with boiled new potatoes (golfball size) and steamed cabbage or perhaps sauerkraut.

♪ Duck and Andouille Gumbo

Andouille or other sausage can be added to thousands of gumbo recipes, and there is some confusion about what's a gumbo and what's not. For the right texture, either okra (the word *gumbo* derives from an African word meaning "okra") or filé powder is necessary. The recipe below calls for okra. (If you use a filé recipe, remember to use it sparingly, at the very end of the cooking, as it can make a stringy mess. In fact, I recommend that filé not be added to the main pot. Instead, ladle hot gumbo into serving bowls. Then stir in the filé to taste. Add a dollop of cooked rice last. In this okra gumbo, however, it is permissible to add gumbo to the rice.)

1 4- to 5-pound duckling
1½ pounds andouille
½ pint freshly shucked oysters
1 cup oyster liquor
1½ cups sliced fresh okra
3 medium onions, chopped
½ cup chopped green onion tops or fresh chives
5 cloves garlic, minced
1 large turnip root, peeled and diced
1 red bell pepper, chopped
¼ cup chopped fresh parsley
3 bay leaves
salt and pepper, to taste
3 to 4 tablespoons flour
hot water
rice (cooked separately)

Pluck, skin, and disjoint the duckling, trimming away any fat. Cut the skin and fat into small pieces, then fry out the oil in a cast-iron stove-top Dutch oven. When most of the oil has been cooked out, what's left of the pieces will be very crisp. These are cracklings. Drain them and set aside. Heat the duck oil to high. Brown and drain the duck pieces. Drain all but about ½ cup of oil from the skillet. Stir 3 or 4 tablespoons of flour into the duck fat. Cook on low, stirring constantly with a wooden spoon, for 30 minutes, or until the mixture (roux) is dark brown. The longer the cooking time, the better, within reason.

Add the chopped onions, green onion tops, bell pepper, okra, parsley, bay leaves, and garlic. Cook for a few minutes. Add the browned duck pieces, along with enough hot water to cover everything. Bring to a light boil, then reduce the heat. Stir in the oyster liquor, along with the salt and pepper. Cover tightly and simmer for 1 hour. In a skillet, brown the sausage pieces, then add them to the pot along with the diced turnip. Cover and simmer for 30 minutes. Add the oysters and simmer for 20 minutes. Serve the gumbo hot over rice, along with a crusty New Orleans sourdough or French bread. Enjoy.

♪ Andouille à la Jeannine

Justin Wilson, the professional Cajun, named this recipe for his wife in *The Justin Wilson Gourmet and Gourmand Cookbook*. In fact, it was the first recipe in what I reckon to be the first chapter of the book, prefaced only by a one-pager on how to make a roux.

2 pounds andouille
1 cup dry white wine
2 tablespoons honey
1 tablespoon Creole mustard

Slice the sausage into ¼- to ½-inch wheels. Place in a skillet. Mix the other ingredients and pour over the sausage. Cover and simmer over low heat for 15 or 20 minutes, or until the sausage is tender. Serve as an appetizer.

Chaurice

Often used in jambalaya and to season various vegetable and bean dishes, chaurice is a hot, spicy pork sausage made with approximately 2 parts lean to 1 part fat. For convenience, I list 7 pounds lean and 3 pounds fat. Usually, however, I use 10 pounds of fatty pork butts without measuring the lean and fat.

7 pounds lean fresh pork, partly frozen

3 pounds pork fat, partly frozen

4 large onions, chopped

4 cloves fresh garlic, minced

3 tablespoons salt

1½ tablespoons freshly ground black pepper

1 tablespoon cayenne (for a hot sausage)

1 tablespoon dried mild red pepper flakes (for color)

1 tablespoon ground allspice

1 tablespoon minced fresh parsley

½ tablespoon minced fresh thyme

1 teaspoon ground bay leaf

sheep or hog casings

Cut the meat into small chunks, mix, and spread out over your work surface. Sprinkle the chopped onions, garlic, parsley, and thyme evenly over the meat. Mix all the spices, then sprinkle over the meat. Grind the meat with a ³⁄₁₆-inch wheel. Make a test patty and fry it in hot lard. Add more black pepper if you want a hotter sausage. If the seasoning suits your taste, stuff the mixture into sheep or hog casings. (Old-time New Orleans Creoles preferred sheep casings, but I usually use medium hog casings because I'm more likely to have them on hand.) Tie the sausages off in convenient lengths.

Use the chaurice in dishes of boiled vegetables, beans, gumbo, or jambalaya. Or eat it by itself if you like a hot, spicy sausage. For best results, deep-fry the links in very hot lard or other cooking oil. Drain and serve.

Sausage and Oyster Jambalaya

The defining ingredients of a true jambalaya, a Spanish-Creole dish akin to the paella, are ham and rice. Since both of these are used in this recipe, I don't have a problem with the name. The sausage and oysters, however, make it special. For best results, use a 13-inch cast-iron jambalaya skillet to cook this recipe. A large stove-top Dutch oven will do.

1 pound smoked pork sausage

1 cup diced fresh lean pork (½-inch cubes)

1 cup diced baked cured ham (½-inch cubes)

1 pint freshly shucked oysters

4 cups chopped onion

4 cloves garlic, minced

1½ cups long-grain white rice

3 cups beef stock

¼ cup butter

½ cup chopped red bell pepper

½ cup chopped green bell pepper

¼ cup chopped green onion tops

¼ cup chopped fresh parsley

1 tablespoon salt

½ teaspoon freshly ground black pepper

½ teaspoon cayenne

½ teaspoon dried thyme

½ teaspoon crushed bay leaf

oyster liquor as needed

Melt the butter in a large skillet or stove-top Dutch oven over medium heat. Sauté the ham, sausage, and pork for 10 minutes or so. Add the onion, green onion tops, peppers, garlic, and parsley. Cook for 30 minutes, stirring from time to time with a wooden spoon. Add the rice. Cook for 5 minutes. Add the beef stock, salt, pepper, cayenne, thyme, and bay leaf. Increase the heat, bringing the liquid to a boil. Add the oysters. Cover and simmer for 1 hour over very low heat. Stir from time to time, being careful not to chop up the oysters. Add a little oyster liquid as needed to keep the dish from drying out. Remove the cover and simmer until the rice dries out a little, stirring gently with a wooden spoon. Serve hot in bowls, along with crusty French bread.

✐ Chaurice with Creole Sauce

I included this recipe in the first draft of this chapter. Later, I took it out because I felt guilty about using too much material from *The Picayune Creole Cook Book*. In the end, I put it back in because I owe it to my readers to publish what I consider to be the best sausage dishes. Besides, it's relatively short whereas most modern Cajun and Creole recipes contain a list of ingredients as long as your leg.

2 pounds chaurice

3 tomatoes, peeled and chopped

1 large onion, chopped

1 clove garlic, minced

1 teaspoon salt

1 teaspoon freshly ground black pepper

½ teaspoon lard

½ cup boiling water

Heat the lard in a cast-iron skillet. Lightly brown the onion. Add the garlic and tomatoes, stirring with a wooden spoon. Prick the sausage links with a fork, then add them to the skillet, cover, and simmer for 5 minutes. Sprinkle with the salt and pepper. Add about ½ cup boiling water. Cover and simmer for 20 minutes. Serve hot for breakfast, along with scrambled eggs and fluffy biscuits.

Picayune Saucisses and Saucissons

According to *The Picayune Creole Cook Cook*, saucisses are sausages made with a mixture of meats—beef, pork, veal, and pork fat. They are made with the same seasonings and technique used for chaurice (above). For a 10-pound batch, try 3 pounds lean pork, 3 pounds beef, 2 pounds veal, and 2 pounds pork fat. For breakfast, saucisses are sliced and deep-fried in fat.

Saucissons are made with beef, pork, and fat—using only the lean tenderloins of beef and pork. To make a 10-pound batch, use the same seasonings listed for chaurice along with 4 pounds fresh beef fillet, 4 pounds fresh pork tenderloin, and 2 pounds pork fat. Use small sheep casings tied in lengths of 3 inches, making a sausage about the size of your little finger. Saucissons are usually fried whole.

Both saucisses and saucissons can be smoked for flavor and make a wonderful ingredient for soups, stews, and rice dishes.

✐ Red Beans, Rice, and Sausage

Traditionally, this dish is made with smoked sausage. In Louisiana, it is often cooked on Monday, the day for washing, and, at one time, the water from the rice was used to starch the clothes before they were ironed. But the dish is good any day of the week, if it is properly made. I like it on a cold day during winter. Here's what you'll need:

2 pounds smoked sausage (in casings)
2 pounds smoked ham hocks
1 pound dried red beans
4 large onions, chopped
6 cloves garlic, minced
salt and pepper, to taste
rice (cooked separately)

Rinse the beans, put them into a suitable pot (preferably a cast-iron Dutch oven) with water, bring to a boil, and cook for 5 minutes. Then turn off the heat and let the beans sit for at least an hour. Pour the water off the beans. Add 3 quarts of fresh water to the beans, then add onions, garlic, and ham hocks. Bring to a boil, reduce heat, cover tightly, and simmer for an hour, or until the beans are tender. Remove the ham hocks and pull off the lean meat, which is put back into the pot. Cut the sausage into 3-inch lengths and add them to the pot. Add a little salt and pepper, to taste. Simmer for 30 minutes, stirring from time to time and adding a little more water if needed. Serve the dish in bowls over rice.

Boudins

Although some modern recipes call for beef blood, a true boudin, sometimes called black pudding, is made with hog blood and fat. According to my old edition of *Larousse Gastronomique,* the addition of blood from other animals "amounts to a fraudulent act!" Moreover, a basic boudin does not call for any lean meat whatsoever, whereas some modern recipes allow fatty pork instead of pure fat. Suit yourself.

✐ Your Basic Creole Boudin

If you don't butcher your own animals, check with your friendly local meat processor for the availability of blood. Substitute beef blood if you must.

2 pints hog blood

1 pound pork fat

3 medium-to-large onions, minced

4 cloves garlic, minced

1 teaspoon crushed dried parsley

1 teaspoon crushed dried thyme

½ teaspoon ground allspice

½ teaspoon ground mace

½ teaspoon ground clove

½ teaspoon ground nutmeg

salt and freshly ground black pepper, to taste

cayenne, to taste

hog casings

Heat a little of the pork fat in a skillet, frying out some grease. Sauté the onion for 5 minutes, stirring often with a wooden spoon. Add the garlic and cook for another 2 or 3 minutes. Set aside. Mix the salt, pepper, cayenne, allspice, mace, clove, parsley, thyme, and nutmeg. Mince the remaining fat. In a suitable container, thoroughly mix the blood, minced fat, and spice mixture. Stuff the mixture into hog casings, making 3-inch links. Place the links in very hot water. Heat but do not boil until the boudins can be pricked without bleeding. Be warned that boiling the boudins will curdle the blood. Dry and cool the boudins, then cook as needed. Refrigerate for a day or two, or freeze for longer storage. Boudins are best when deep-fried in lard, but they can also be grilled or broiled.

✐ Johnson's Boudin Blanc

Adapted from *Tony Chachere's Cajun Country Cookbook,* this recipe makes an excellent white boudin. Note that rice is an essential ingredient, helping to give the sausage a white color. Other recipes for boudin blanc (mostly French) call for cream—lots of cream—and chicken eggs as well as pork fat, making them very rich as well as high in fat.

3 pounds lean fresh pork
1 pound pork fat
1 pound pork liver
1 medium onion, chopped
1 green bell pepper, chopped
2 stalks celery with tops, chopped
2 cloves garlic, minced
1 cup chopped green onion tops
½ cup chopped fresh parsley
cooked rice
Tony's Creole Seasoning
hog casings

Trim, dice, and mix the meats, vegetables, and parsley, spreading the mixture over your countertop or worktable. Sprinkle with Tony's Creole Seasoning. Grind the mixture in a sausage mill, using a ⅛-inch wheel. Measure the mixture, counting the cups. To each cup of mixture, add 2 cups cooked rice. Mix well. If the mixture seems too dry, add a little water. Stuff the mixture into medium or large hog casings, linking every 6 or 8 inches. Bring a large pot of water to a rolling boil. Place the sausage into the water and boil gently for 30 minutes. Refrigerate until needed.

Variation for Leftovers. During my boyhood in the country, we always had a huge turkey and fresh pork for both Thanksgiving and

Christmas. I also ate the same fare with relatives. In short, I was turned off by leftovers before the holiday season was over. Boudin blanc sausages make a good way out. Just substitute leftover turkey or cooked fresh ham, or both, for the fresh pork in the above recipe.

6

German and Austrian Sausages

Being the home of the world-famous frankfurter would be enough to establish Germany in the history of foods. Germans love sausage; in fact, they eat more pounds of sausage per year than any other people. They like not only quantity but also variety. From the Middle Ages to modern times, Germany has been the center of the commercial sausage industry. Over fifteen hundred different kinds of *wursts* have been developed in Germany, where in times past the local *wurst-macher*, usually with a secret recipe, often grew rich and powerful. Today sausage eating is a traditional part of the annual Oktoberfest, not only in Munich but also in the German communities in Texas and Wisconsin.

The popular frankfurter (also called wiener or hot dog) is covered in Chapter 15, leaving mostly the *wursts* to be covered here. It's impossible to cover all these in a short book, but here are my favorites.

Bratwurst

This pale, mildly seasoned sausage is usually made with a combination of pork and veal; proportions vary, but 2 parts pork to 1 part veal is the norm. It is stuffed in medium hog casings, tied off in 6-inch links.

7 pounds pork butt or shoulder

3 pounds veal

2 tablespoons salt

1 tablespoon white pepper

2 teaspoons caraway seed

2 teaspoons dried marjoram

2 teaspoons ground allspice

1¾ cups ice water

medium hog casings

Cut the pork and veal into chunks. Mix and spread out over your work surface. Combine all the spices, mix well, and sprinkle evenly over the meats. Grind with a ³⁄₁₆- or ⅛-inch plate. Mix in the ice water with your hands. Stuff into hog casings. Dry the casing surface and refrigerate.

Typically, links of bratwurst are cooked for a few minutes in boiling water or broth, then dipped into milk or cream and broiled or grilled. They are also panfried in butter. When you make a batch, be sure to make some patties to cook on the griddle. See also the recipes below.

Texas Bratwurst

The German immigrants around New Braunfels, Texas, take their sausage seriously, and thousands of pounds are grilled during annual festivals. Here's an excellent recipe that I have adapted from *The Only Texas Cookbook,* by Linda West Eckhardt. Be sure to try this one, especially if you want to use lean pork.

5 pounds lean pork (try loin)

5 pounds lean veal

2 cups soft white bread crumbs

1 cup milk

2 tablespoons salt

4 teaspoons dried sage

2 teaspoons white pepper

3 cups ice water

hog casings

Cut the meats into chunks, mix, and spread out over your work surface. Sprinkle evenly with the salt, sage, and white pepper. Grind the meats twice with a ⅛- or ³⁄₁₆-inch plate. Soak the bread crumbs in milk, then, using your hands, mix them with the sausage meats. Mix in the water and beat until light and fluffy. Stuff into hog casings, tying off in 6-inch links. Either cook right away or freeze.

To cook the bratwurst Texas-style, place some links into a skillet with enough salted water to cover. (An electric skillet works fine.) Bring to a boil, lower the heat, and simmer for 10 minutes. Dry the sausages, then roll them in flour and sauté in butter. When the bratwurst is nicely browned, remove to a serving platter. Add a little dry white wine to the skillet, scraping up any pan drippings, and simmer until you have a nice gravy. Serve the bratwurst topped with fried onions, along with the gravy and mashed potatoes.

✍ Creamed Bratwurst

Here's a dish that I like to cook whenever I happen upon edible wild mushrooms along the way. Puffballs will do, but morels or chanterelles are better. If you don't eat wild mushrooms, try store-bought shiitakes or sliced portobellos.

¾ to 1 pound bratwurst

2 cups half-and-half

1 cup sliced mushrooms

1 cup chopped onion

¼ cup chopped fresh parsley

2 tablespoons butter

2 tablespoons flour

salt and white pepper, to taste

Heat some water in a pot and simmer the bratwurst links for about

15 minutes, until cooked through. Cool and slice the bratwurst into ½-inch wheels. Heat the butter in a skillet. Sauté the onion, mushrooms, and parsley for 5 or 6 minutes. Stir in the flour along with a little salt and white pepper to taste. Pour in the half-and-half and cook, stirring as you go, until the mixture is bubbly but not boiling. Stir in the bratwurst pieces and simmer for 2 or 3 minutes. Serve over toast.

Bockwurst

This small delicate sausage is made from veal and pork, flavored with onion, clove, and parsley. The mix of meats can vary considerably, ranging from 9 parts veal to 1 part pork fat. I like it made with half veal and half fatty pork, as from the butt or shoulder. Traditionally, bockwurst is made in the spring, during *bockbier* time, when the dark bock beer is ready.

5 pounds pork butt or shoulder
5 pounds veal
5 cups milk
8 chicken eggs, lightly whisked
2 large onions, chopped
2 tablespoons salt
2 tablespoons white pepper
2 tablespoons sugar
2 tablespoons minced dried parsley
½ tablespoon ground clove
¼ tablespoon minced dried sage
¼ tablespoon ground mace
small hog casings

Cut the meat into chunks, mix with the onions, and spread it over your work surface. Sprinkle evenly with the sage, mace, salt, pepper, sugar, clove, and parsley. Grind with a ⅛-inch plate, or grind twice with a ³⁄₁₆-inch plate. Mix in the milk and chicken eggs. Stuff in small hog casings or perhaps sheep casings, tying off in 3- or 4-inch links. Heat some water in a large pot. Simmer the bockwurst for 10 minutes. Dry the surface. Cook immediately, refrigerate for a day or two, or freeze. To cook, sauté the links in butter along with some chopped onions. Serve hot.

Variation: Add the juice of 3 or 4 lemons before stuffing the bockwurst into the casings.

♪ Bavarian Salad

Here's a recipe that I adapted from *The New German Cookbook* by Jean Anderson and Hedy Würz. The authors say that Bavarians make it with bockwurst, but that they substituted bologna because it is easier to obtain here in America. It's better, however, to make your own bockwurst. Cook the bockwurst by simmering it in water for about 10 minutes. Also, the authors list corn oil in the ingredients. I have changed this to olive oil.

2 pounds bockwurst, simmered

2 medium onions, chopped

½ cup olive oil

¼ cup red wine vinegar

1 tablespoon brown mustard

salt and freshly ground black pepper, to taste

2 tablespoons chopped fresh chives

2 tablespoons chopped fresh flat-leaf parsley

Cut the bockwurst into bite-size chunks. Mix with the onions in a large bowl. In a small bowl, mix the oil, red wine vinegar, mustard, salt, and pepper. Whisk until creamy. Pour the oil mix over the bockwurst and onions, toss, cover, and marinate in the refrigerator for 2 hours. When you are ready to serve, toss in the chives and parsley.

Knockwurst

This hefty sausage can be stuffed into large hog casings or small beef rounds.

7 pounds beef

3 pounds fatty fresh pork

10 cloves garlic, minced

6 tablespoons salt

5 tablespoons white pepper

4 tablespoons sugar

2 tablespoons Hungarian paprika

1 tablespoon ground mace

½ tablespoon ground coriander

2 cups ice water

large hog casings or small beef rounds

Cut the beef and pork into chunks, mix, and spread over your work surface. Mix all the dry ingredients, then sprinkle them evenly over the meat, along with the minced garlic. Grind the meat with a ⅛-inch plate, or grind twice with a ³⁄₁₆-inch plate. Mix in the ice water, working the mass with your hands. Stuff into large hog casings or small beef rounds. Dry the surface and cold-smoke for an hour or so. Cook immediately or freeze.

Knockwurst is usually baked or fried in a skillet. In the latter case, I usually simmer mine first before frying to make sure it is cooked thoroughly. Cooking times will vary with the thickness of the sausage. If in doubt, use a meat thermometer. The center of a representative link should read at least 152 degrees F. Note that the sausage can be taken directly from the smoker and grilled over charcoal, or it can be cooked in the smoker by increasing the heat. Also see the Knockwurst with Beer recipe, next.

Knockwurst with Beer

I would like to say that I wrestled this recipe from a plump German chef during Oktoberfest, but in truth I have adapted it from *The New York Times Cookbook,* put together by Craig Claiborne. I don't know what sort of beer Claiborne used, but I tried it with dark Lowenbrau.

8 knockwurst links

1 pint German beer

2 tablespoon vinegar

2 teaspoons sugar

Heat the beer in a saucepan, add the knockwurst, and simmer on very low heat for 15 minutes. (If the knockwurst are thick, perhaps stuffed in beef rounds, increase the cooking time to 20 minutes.) Place the cooked knockwurst onto a heated broiling pan. Preheat the broiler. Increase the heat under the saucepan, boiling and stirring until the beer stock is reduced to about ⅓ cup. Stir in the vinegar and sugar. Stir. Pour the resulting sauce over the knockwurst. Broil for a few minutes, turning to brown both sides. Serve hot.

Mettwurst

This mild German sausage, made of fresh pork and pork liver, is similar to liverwurst. It makes a wonderful sandwich. Mettwurst recipes abound, however, and some of these do not call for liver or for cooking. In my version, the fresh pork and liver are cooked before grinding and the whole sausage is simmered in salted water, then refrigerated. This sausage is difficult to slice because it tends to fall apart. I do, however, slice it when made in hog casings. With larger casings, I break the sausage apart with a fork and mix it with mayonnaise as a sandwich spread. Some recipes make a soft mettwurst (also called teewurst), which is used as a spread and is considered a tea sausage.

6 pounds fresh pork
4 pounds fresh pork liver
salted water
¼ cup salt
2 tablespoons white pepper
2 tablespoons ground coriander
unsalted cold water
beef rounds or large hog casings

Cut the pork and liver into chunks. Simmer in lightly salted water for about 30 minutes. Cool the meat, then spread it out on your work surface and sprinkle evenly with salt, white pepper, and coriander. Grind and stuff into beef rounds or perhaps large hog casings. Simmer in lightly salted water for 30 minutes (20 minutes or less for hog casings, depending on size). Chill in cold water, dry the surface, and refrigerate for up to 2 weeks, using as needed as a sandwich filler or cracker spread. Freeze for longer storage.

Gehirnwurst

Brains have always been one of my favorite meats, and I was therefore gustatorily aroused when I first ran across a cryptic version of this recipe in an old edition of *Larousse Gastronomique*.

5 pounds pork brains

3 pounds lean pork

2 pounds pork fat

2 tablespoons freshly ground black pepper

1 tablespoon ground mace

5 tablespoons salt

hog casings

Heat a pot of water and simmer the pork brains for about 10 minutes. Drain and cut the brains into chunks. Also cut the pork and fat into chunks. Mix the brains, fat, pork, pepper, mace, and salt on your work surface. Grind with a 3/16-inch plate. Stuff into hog casings, tying off every 8 inches or so. To cook, poach in water for 5 minutes, then sauté, preferably in butter. Either cook or freeze gehirnwurst right away.

Vienna Sausage

This Austrian specialty is made from beef and pork, sometimes with veal added. Onion, mace, and coriander are the dominant seasonings. Stuffed into sheep casings, the Vienna sausage is similar to the frankfurter (Chapter 15), but is a little shorter and not quite as fat.

6 pounds pork butt or shoulder

4 pounds lean beef

2 cups cold milk

1 cup flour

½ cup chopped onion

3 tablespoons salt

2 tablespoons ground coriander

1 tablespoon sugar

1 tablespoon ground mace

1 tablespoon Hungarian paprika

½ tablespoon cayenne

sheep casings

Cut the beef and pork into chunks suitable for grinding. Mix these on your work surface and sprinkle evenly with the coriander, salt, sugar, mace, paprika, cayenne, and chopped onion. (The spices can be mixed before sprinkling over the meat.) Grind with a ³⁄₁₆-inch plate; then grind twice with a ⅛-inch plate. Thoroughly mix in the milk and flour. Stuff the mix into sheep casings, tying off every 4 inches. Place the links into a large pot and cover with water. Bring to a boil, then reduce the heat and simmer (do not allow it to boil again) for 45 minutes. Remove the links, cool, dry the surface, and refrigerate or freeze. (These can also be canned, but I don't recommend the practice.) Before eating, reheat the sausages in boiling water or, better, grill over charcoal or a wood fire.

Italian Sausages

I taly is the home of some of the world's most popular sausage, including bologna, salami, and pepperoni. Since these three are popular as cold cuts and sandwich meats in America and other parts of the world, I have covered them in Chapter 15. Don't worry. There's still enough good eating left to distinguish Italy in the world of sausage. It all started long ago.

Ancient Roman Sausage

Apicius, the ancient culinary sport, gave us the work *Cookery and Dining in Imperial Rome*—our oldest extant cookbook. The Romans adopted the sausage from the ancient Greeks, who had a profound influence on the food and cookery of southern Italy and Sicily. In addition to making their own, the Romans also imported tons of cured sausage and ham from the Gauls. In any case, Apicius left us several sausages. By today's standards, the recipes are rather cryptic, lacking complete instructions and measurements. The recipes below are reconstructed as best I can make out. The inquisitive scholar might want to take a look at the Latin text or a translation. A translation of the whole work has been reprinted by Dover Publications, and other translations are no doubt available.

Meanwhile, notice that the sample recipes below are very close to a modern sausage. But none of the original recipes listed salt or any sort of cure. Beware. My guess is that it never occurred to Apicius to list salt as an ingredient, as any fool would know to add salt to fresh pork. Salt was very much in demand in the Roman Empire, and, in fact, our word for salt derived from the Latin word meaning "salary." It has even been argued that the word *sausage* is derived from *salt*.

Lucanian Sausage

Mince some fresh pork. Add crushed pepper, cumin, savory, chopped parsley, and broth. Pound the mixture. Add some whole peppercorns and nuts. Stuff into casings and hang to smoke. The original recipe also called for rue, laurel berries, and "condiment." Since I don't know exactly what these are in modern culinary terms, I have left them out. The "nuts" could have been any of several, but my guess is that pine nuts were the favorite. In any case, if the recipe is made with reasonable amounts of meat and spices, it will be perfectly acceptable today. Try simmering the links for 15 minutes, then frying them.

Apicius has a recipe for sautéing sausage with the white part of chopped leeks, serving them with a wine sauce. I can't piece together the sauce recipe, but a translator's footnote speculates that the recipe came from Tarentum, a town of southern Italy noted for its wine and luxurious living. Anyhow, the sausage and chopped leeks is a very good sauté.

Ancient Brain Sausage

Poach the brains in a little water until cooked. Mix with raw chicken eggs, pine nuts, pepper, broth, and a little laser. (Laser was a very popular ancient wild herb. It was in great demand, and, being picked too frequently, may now be extinct.) Stuff the mixture into hog casings. Simmer in water for a few minutes, then sauté or fry.

Since brains and eggs (scrambled together) are one of my favorite foods, I have cooked this recipe several times, using various leafy herbs in lieu of laser. Ordinary parsley will do. This sausage is very good, and these days brains are one of the best nutritional values available at our supermarkets and meat shops.

Spelt Sausage

Spelt is an ancient wheatlike grain and is still available today. (I purchase whole spelt berries from King Arthur Flour company, listed in Sources, page 193.) Any hard wheat berry will do. First, cook the spelt or wheat berries in stock until tender. (It helps to soak the berries overnight in water.) Chop some bacon and *hot* fat (from around the innards) and fresh pork. Mix with the cooked spelt berries, crushed pepper, lovage, chicken eggs, pine nuts, and broth. Pound with a mortar and pestle. Stuff the mixture into hog casings. Poach in water for 20 minutes, then serve hot. These sausages can also be poached and fried or grilled. The Apicius text is a little unclear but notes from translators indicate that this sausage was served with pheasant gravy flavored with cumin.

In any case, I hope that this recipe will introduce a few readers to spelt and wheat berries. They can be used in soups and stews, adding a delightful change of texture as well as taste and will boost the recipes' nutritional value tremendously. Why we Americans have neglected this healthful food is a cultural mystery to me.

Sweet Italian Sausage

Fennel dominates the seasonings in this mild sausage. I prefer to measure out the seeds, then crush them on a suitable surface with the flat side of a meat mallet. Most recipes, however, merely specify seeds. Suit yourself.

10 pounds pork butt or shoulder
2 cups good red wine
10 cloves garlic, minced
2 tablespoons salt
2 tablespoons fennel seed
1½ tablespoons white pepper

1 tablespoon dried sage

hog casings

Cut the meat into chunks suitable for grinding. Spread the meat out on your work surface. Sprinkle evenly with the dry seasonings and garlic. Grind with a ³⁄₁₆-inch plate. Work the wine into the ground meat. Stuff in hog casings or use as bulk sausage—or try half one way and half the other.

To cook, fry or bake. The stuffed sausages should be poached for about 15 minutes before frying in a little olive oil. This sausage can be refrigerated for several days, or frozen for longer storage.

A. D.'s Eggplant Parmigiana

This combination of tomato, eggplant, bulk Italian sausage, and Italian cheeses is one of my favorite dishes. Although the ingredient list below calls for flour, I sometimes dust the eggplant in fine stone-ground white cornmeal.

1 large eggplant

1 pound bulk Italian mild sausage

2 cups chopped Italian tomatoes

2 cups tomato sauce

1 cup chopped onion

5 cloves garlic, minced

1 cup freshly grated mozzarella cheese

½ cup freshly grated Parmesan cheese

flour, for dusting

olive oil

salt, to taste

pepper, to taste

Preheat the oven to 375 degrees F and grease a shallow baking dish of about 8 by 12 inches. Peel the eggplant and cut it into ¼- to ½-inch slices. Sprinkle the slices on both sides with salt, then spread them out over absorbent paper. Heat a little olive oil in a skillet. Sauté the onion and garlic for 5 or 6 minutes. Add the tomatoes and tomato sauce, stirring and heating through, adding salt and pepper to taste. In another skillet or saucepan, heat a little olive oil and sauté the sausage for a few minutes. Drain and mix the sausage into the tomato and onions. If needed, heat a little more olive oil. Pat the eggplant slices dry and sprinkle on both sides with flour, shaking off the excess. Sauté the eggplant slices until they are golden on both sides. Spread a little of the tomato-sausage mixture over the bottom of the baking dish. Cover with eggplant slices and a layer of both cheeses. Add another layer of tomato sauce, eggplant, and cheeses. End with tomato sauce. Sprinkle lightly with olive oil. Cover the dish and bake for 30 minutes. Uncover and bake for another 15 minutes or so. Serve hot with plenty of crusty Italian bread, lots of fresh tossed salad, and vino.

Luganega

I've seen several recipes for Sicilian or Italian sausage made with the aid of a grated dry cheese and wine. Some of these call for vermouth or chablis, but I say that a dry red wine is in order. I won't insist on chianti, but it is a good choice and is usually readily available in America. Suit yourself. In any case, this recipe (and the name of the sausage) has been adapted from *The Sausage-Making Cookbook,* by Jerry Predika (who specifies dry vermouth). Rytek Kutas set forth a similar recipe in his *Great Sausage Recipes and Meat Curing,* listing Romano cheese and chablis wine; this, he said, is his favorite Italian sausage. In *Home Sausage Making,* Charles G. Reavis calls luganega unique because it is flavored with freshly grated lemon and orange zest. I might add that other sausages are flavored with orange or lemon peel, and in Catalonia zest of the bitter Seville orange is used. In any case, I consider the wine and cheese to be the distinguishing ingredients.

10 pounds pork butt

3 cups grated Parmesan cheese

2 cups dry vermouth

2 cloves garlic, minced

2 tablespoons salt

1 tablespoon freshly ground black pepper

1½ teaspoons ground nutmeg

1½ teaspoons ground coriander
1 teaspoon freshly grated orange zest
1 teaspoon freshly grated lemon zest
hog casings

Cut the meat into chunks suitable for grinding. Mix the salt, pepper, coriander, and nutmeg, sprinkling the mixture evenly over the meat. Grind it with a ³⁄₁₆-inch plate. Mix in the garlic, orange zest, lemon zest, cheese, and wine. Stuff into hog casings. Cook immediately or freeze. (Freezing will alter the flavor somewhat.) Use in soups and stews, or poach for 15 minutes and then fry or grill.

✎ Tuscan Beans with Sausage

Dean & Deluca, the New York mail-order outfit, specifies Jacob's cattle beans for this recipe. These are large, quick-cooking beans and I highly recommend them not only for taste and texture but also for color. Substitute calypso beans if you have them on hand. In Italy, Tuscans are called *mangiafagiole*, meaning "bean eaters." This recipe goes a long way toward justification of the predilection.

1 pound luganega
½ pound Jacob's cattle beans
1 large onion, chopped
2 large tomatoes, chopped
1 teaspoon chopped fresh rosemary
1 teaspoon chopped fresh sage
salt and freshly ground black pepper, to taste

Rinse the beans. Simmer them in a pot, well covered with water, for 1 hour. Remove the pot from the heat but leave the beans in the hot water as you proceed. Place the sausage in a large skillet. Add enough water to measure 1 inch. Cook the sausage uncovered until almost all the water has evaporated, leaving the grease that will have cooked out of the sausage. Add the onion and cook for 5 minutes. Remove the sausage, slice into 1-inch pieces, and set aside. Add the tomatoes, sage, rosemary, salt, and pepper to the onions. Cover and simmer on low heat for 10 minutes. Add the sausage pieces and cooked beans. Cover and simmer for 5 minutes. Serve hot, along with crusty bread and red vino.

Coteghino

This excellent sausage, usually rather large, calls for pork and pork skin with the fat attached. It's easy to use a fresh ham, cutting the meat and skin as needed. Stuff the sausage into small beef rounds or large hog casings.

7 pounds pork

3 pounds pork skin with fat

1 cup grated Parmesan cheese

4 cloves garlic, minced

6 tablespoons salt

3 tablespoons freshly ground black pepper

1 tablespoon ground nutmeg

1 tablespoon ground cinnamon

1 tablespoon cayenne

1 teaspoon ground clove

2 cups cold water

hog casings or beef rounds

Cut the pork and skin into chunks suitable for grinding. Spread the chunks over the work surface, mixing well. Sprinkle the spices evenly over the pork, then grind with a ³⁄₁₆-inch plate. Mix in the Parmesan, garlic, and water, working with your hands. Stuff the mixture into small beef rounds or large hog casings, tying off with twine in 8-inch lengths, leaving a loop on one end. Hang the links in a cool, breezy place for 4 or 5 days before cooking. If you don't have a suitable place, clean out a section of your refrigerator and hang the links. To cook, simmer the links in water for 1½ hours. Prick the links with a fork while cooking. Traditionally, these sausages are served with lentils.

Note: Some coteghino recipes call for saltpeter. This ingredient will give the coteghino a reddish color, but I elect to leave it out. If you want it, use ⅓ teaspoon for the recipe, and be sure to mix it very evenly into the salt and other dry ingredients. Also see the text in Chapter 3. Going the other way, another recipe calls for a greatly reduced quantity of salt, which I can't recommend. In any case, remember that the recipe above is not for a fully cured sausage. It should be treated as a fresh sausage. In other words, it should be either cooked right away, refrigerated for a few days, or frozen for longer storage.

8

British Isle Sausages

The British Isles are more noted for meat pies than for sausages, and cows or sheep are probably more important than hogs. Still, the sausage is popular for breakfast, especially bulk patties, and sometimes cooked in beans and other dishes.

Bulk Country Sausage with Watercress

This recipe calls for lean pork butts, but the mix can be made with 80 percent lean pork, as from the loin, and 20 percent fat. If you start off with a butt that contains too much fat, trim it a little. Often country sausage is made with lots of fresh herbs, making it the ideal sausage for home gardeners.

10 pounds pork butt, on the lean side

4 cups minced fresh parsley

4 cups minced green onions with tops

4 cups minced watercress

¼ **cup minced fresh marjoram**

¼ **cup minced fresh rosemary**

¼ **cup minced fresh tarragon**

¼ **cup minced fresh thyme**

¼ **cup rubbed dried sage**

6 **tablespoons sea salt or kosher salt**

2 **tablespoons caraway seed**

1 **tablespoon freshly ground black pepper**

Cut the meat into chunks, spread it out on your work surface, and sprinkle it evenly with the spices and herbs. Grind with a ³⁄₁₆-inch plate. Mix again with your hands and shape into patties. Either cook the patties right away or wrap tightly in foil and freeze. Note that frozen patties can be pan-grilled successfully or sautéed without thawing.

Bangers

Here's an old English sausage made with pork, seasonings, and crumbled stale biscuits. Stale bread can be substituted. The recipe also calls for chilled pork stock. If this is a problem, use ice water, chilled beef broth, or perhaps chicken stock.

8 **pounds lean pork**

2 **pounds pork fat**

2½ **pounds stale biscuits**

7 **cups chilled pork stock**

6 **tablespoons salt**

1 **tablespoon white pepper**

½ **tablespoon ground mace**

½ **tablespoon ground ginger**

¼ **tablespoon dried sage**

hog casings

Cut the meat and fat into chunks suitable for grinding. Spread the meat on your work surface, mix well, and sprinkle evenly with the spices. Grind the mix with a ³⁄₁₆-inch plate. Crumble the biscuits and soak them in a little of the stock. Mix the meat, biscuits, and stock.

Stuff into hog casings, tying off in convenient lengths. Hang in a cool, airy place for 24 hours. Cook immediately, refrigerate for a day or two, or freeze. These sausages, popular for breakfast, can be simmered, broiled, grilled, baked, or fried.

Oxford Sausage

This delicious sausage is made with a mix of fatty pork, veal, and beef, seasoned with various spices and lemon zest. When grating the lemon, use a fine mesh and be careful to avoid the bitter white pith.

4 pounds fatty pork, such as butt or shoulder

4 pounds veal

2 pounds lean beef

crumbs from 1 loaf sourdough bread

8 chicken eggs, whisked

zest of 3 lemons

3 tablespoons salt

1½ teaspoons freshly ground black pepper

2 teaspoons dried sage

2 teaspoons dried thyme

2 teaspoons dried rosemary

2 teaspoons grated nutmeg

2 teaspoons dried minced savory

2 cups ice water

medium hog casings

Cut the meat into chunks suitable for grinding, mix, and sprinkle evenly with the dry spices. Grind with a ³⁄₁₆-inch plate. Mix in the lemon zest, bread crumbs, chicken eggs, and ice water. Mix thoroughly. Stuff into medium hog casings. Cook, refrigerate for a day or two, or freeze. To cook, fry in a little cooking oil, broil, or grill. I like to simmer these for about 15 minutes in water, then dry and sauté or broil them. When frying, add a little water to the skillet so that the sausage is partly steamed.

Black Pudding

This English blood sausage is distinguished by rice that has been cooked separately and mixed into the pork. Sometimes cooked barley or oatmeal is used instead of, or in addition to, the rice.

1 quart very fresh pig or beef blood

2 pounds pork fat

1½ pounds uncooked rice

⅓ pint heavy cream

4 chicken eggs

2 cups chopped onion

2 tablespoons salt

1 tablespoon freshly ground black pepper

1 tablespoon celery seed

1 tablespoon ground coriander

1 tablespoon dry mustard

½ tablespoon dried thyme

2 bay leaves, ground

hot water

beef rounds or muslin bags

Cook the rice according to the directions on the package. Chop the pork fat into ¼-inch dice. Heat the pork fat in a skillet until a little grease cooks out. Take up the pork fat, then sauté the onion in the grease for 5 or 6 minutes. Mix the blood, eggs, pork fat, rice, onion, cream, spices, and seasonings. Stuff the mixture loosely into beef rounds or perhaps muslin bags, tying off in 8-inch links. Simmer the sausage in very hot (but not boiling) water for 40 minutes. Maintain the water temperature at about 200 degrees F so that the black pudding will cook through. Prick the skin of a sausage. If no blood oozes out, it is done. Keep an eye on the links while poaching. Prick those that rise to the surface, letting the air escape to prevent bursting. Cool the links. To cook, slice the links and grill over charcoal, or slice and fry. Serve hot with applesauce.

Irish Sausage

This pork sausage is traditionally stuffed into sheep casings. Substitute small hog casings if they are more convenient. The pork should contain about 30 percent fat; the typical pork butt or shoulder will do just fine.

10 pounds fatty pork

10 cups bread crumbs

8 chicken eggs, whisked

15 to 20 cloves garlic, minced

3 tablespoons salt

1 tablespoon freshly ground black pepper

1 tablespoon dried thyme

1 tablespoon dried basil

1 tablespoon dried rosemary

1 tablespoon dried marjoram

4 cups cold water

sheep casings

Cut the pork into chunks suitable for grinding, spread it out on your work surface, sprinkle it evenly with the herbs and spices, and grind it with a 3/16-inch plate. Mix the ground meat with the cold water, eggs, and bread crumbs, then stuff the mixture into sheep casings. Cook right away, refrigerate for a day or so, or freeze. These are best when sautéed in butter.

Dublin Coddle

I found this recipe, and the name for it, in *Traditional Irish Recipes,* a quaint little book by George L. Thomson. The format has been changed; the recipe rewritten.

The Stew

8 links Irish pork sausage

8 slices ham (¼- inch thick)

4 pounds Irish potatoes

4 large onions

4 tablespoons chopped fresh parsley

salt and pepper, to taste

Cut the ham slices into bite-size pieces. Simmer the ham pieces and sausage in 1 quart of water for 5 minutes. Drain the ham and sausage, saving the stock. Put the ham and sausage into a pot along with the potatoes, onions, parsley, salt, and pepper. Barely cover with the stock. Bring to a boil, then reduce the heat to very low. Cover with grease-proof paper, then cover with the lid and simmer for 1 hour. Serve hot with freshly made Irish soda bread and stout.

The Soda Bread

1 pound flour

½ pint buttermilk

½ teaspoon baking soda

½ teaspoon salt

Preheat the oven to 400 degrees F. Sift the flour into a bowl, mixing in the soda and salt. Make a hole in the middle of the flour, then add the buttermilk. Stir with a wooden spoon until you have a soft dough. Flour your hands and knead the dough lightly. Place the dough on a floured board, then flatten it into a circle about 1½ inches thick. Place on a cast-iron griddle. Using a knife, make a cross on top of the dough, centering it precisely. Bake for 40 minutes. Break the bread into four pieces (along the lines of the cross) and serve hot with the stew and stout.

Scotch-Irish Eggs

Hard-boiled chicken eggs encased with breakfast sausage make a tasty lunch or brunch, especially suited for wayfarers and hikers. Because the recipe has been attributed to both Scotland and Ireland, I call them Scotch-Irish eggs.

oil for deep-frying

6 large hard-boiled chicken eggs

1 tablespoon flour

salt and pepper, if needed

1 pound breakfast sausage (bulk)

2 raw chicken eggs

1 cup dried bread crumbs

Rig for deep-frying. Shell the hard-boiled eggs. Mix the flour, salt, and pepper into the sausage, then divide into 6. Pat each part into a thin roundish patty, just wide enough to encase a hard boiled egg. Carefully wrap each egg with a patty, distributing the sausage as evenly as possible. Beat the 2 raw eggs in a bowl and put the bread crumbs into a plate. Dip each sausage-encased boiled egg in the beaten egg, then roll it in the bread crumbs, coating evenly all around. Deep-fry the eggs in hot oil (350 degrees F) for 3 or 4 minutes. Unless you have a very large deep-fryer, it will be best to cook the eggs in more than one batch. Remove the eggs with a large slotted spoon and drain on a brown paper bag. Eat warm or cold. If properly wrapped, the eggs will keep half a day without refrigeration. These will freeze nicely.

Highland Haggis

Some recipes for haggis are just too long to be realistic, almost as if the authors of the recipes were trying to hide the essential ingredients. Here's a short version, closer, I think, to the original Highland recipe.

1 sheep stomach

salt for soaking stomach

1 sheep liver

1 sheep heart

1 set sheep kidneys

1 set sheep sweetbreads (if you can find them among the innards)

½ pound fat, diced

1 cup oatmeal

1 large onion, grated

milk

salt and pepper, to taste

Clean and soak the stomach in salted water (1 box salt per gallon of water) overnight. When you are ready to proceed, simmer the heart and kidneys for 1½ hours in a pot; cool and trim away the pipes and gristle. Cut the cooked heart and kidneys into chunks. Cut the liver and sweetbreads into chunks. Mix all the meats and fat, along with the grated onion, oatmeal, salt, and pepper. Run the mixture through a sausage mill, using a ¼- to ½-inch plate. Add a little water to the mixture, working it with your hands. Stuff the mixture into the stomach, leaving some room for the oatmeal to expand. Sew up the opening with cotton twine. Place the stuffed stomach into a pot of suitable size, add enough water and milk to almost cover it, and bring to a boil. Prick the stomach here and there as soon as it begins to swell. Simmer for 3 hours. Serve the haggis plain with straight Scotch whiskey.

9

French Sausages

I n ancient times the region of Europe known as Gaul, with France as its heart, contained sprawling forests of oak and beech trees. On the beechnuts and sweet acorns pigs foraged, with an occasional truffle going to the best sniffers. As soon as the word got out that these acorn-fed hogs were of excellent quality, the Gauls started exporting cured hams and sausages to the Romans in large quantities.

In time, the *charcuterie* trade became highly regulated under various governmental rules and restrictions, explaining, I think, the decline of the homemade French sausage. For whatever reason, modern French cookbooks may give a few recipes for cooking *with* a variety of sausages, but they offer no directions for actually *making* them, leaving this task to the professional *charcutiers*. My old edition of *The Escoffier Cook Book*, for example, sets forth fewer than ten recipes that I consider to be about sausages (or how to cook with them), whereas it contains—in telling contrast—well over one hundred recipes for sauces of one sort or another. Of the sausage recipes five are for "puddings," as Escoffier called blood sausages, or boudins. In addition to the puddings, he gives us two recipes for crépinettes—seasoned ground meat wrapped in caul fat and fried—which may or may not be a sausage, depending on your definition. Of the other three recipes, the first is merely a condescending statement, to wit, "The most known sausages of many nations are cooked like the French kind, and are often served at breakfasts as an accompaniment to bacon. . . . Their seasoning is often excessive." One of the remaining two Escoffier recipes tells us how to cook Frankfort and Strasburg sausages (poach for no longer than 10 minutes and serve with grated horseradish, applesauce, or braised sauerkraut).

Predictably, Escoffier's final recipe tells us how to cook sausages with the aid of wine. Although the recipe is short enough at first glance, it calls for ⅙ pint of half-glaze, recipe 23. That's where the trouble starts. To make a half-glaze, Escoffier says, we'll need, along with some excellent sherry, 1 quart of Espagnole sauce, recipe 22, page 18, and 1 quart of Brown Stock, recipe 7, pages 9 and 10. Astoundingly, recipe 7 for Brown Stock calls for the following: 4 pounds shin of beef, 4 pounds shin of veal, ½ pound raw ham, ½ pound fresh pork rind, blanched, ¾ pound minced carrots browned in butter, ¾ pound minced onion browned in butter, and 1 herb bunch containing a little parsley, a stalk of celery, a small sprig of thyme, and a bay leaf. I don't know what we need to make the Espagnole sauce proper, as I didn't get that far. All I wanted to do was cook a link or two of sausage!

Nonetheless, I have puzzled out a few French creations, starting with a spice mix that can be used in several recipes. Also, some modified French sausage recipes were set forth Chapter 5.

Quatre Épices

This French blend, sometimes available commercially, is often used in sausages and pâtés. You can mix your own easily enough.

5 teaspoons ground white pepper
1 teaspoon ground ginger
1 teaspoon freshly grated nutmeg
½ teaspoon ground clove
½ teaspoon ground cinnamon

Grind and thoroughly mix all the spices. Store in a jar, tightly closed, in a cool, dark place. The measures set forth above can easily be doubled or increased tenfold.

Chipolata

This recipe for this excellent French sausage has been adapted from *Meat Book,* by Jack Ubaldi. It's a small sausage and should be stuffed into sheep casings. Small hog casings will do.

5 pounds pork butt or shoulder
2½ pounds fresh pork belly
2½ pounds boned veal neck
1¼ pounds chopped onion
3½ ounces salt
3 teaspoons coarsely ground pepper
3 cloves garlic, minced
1½ teaspoons Quatre Épices
sheep casings

Cut the meat into chunks, spread it out on your work surface, and sprinkle evenly with the onion, garlic, and seasonings. Grind the mixture with a ⅛-inch plate, or twice with a ³⁄₁₆-inch plate. Stuff the mixture into sheep casings, tying off into 3- to 4-inch links. Panfry for breakfast or use in casseroles and other well-cooked dishes. Refrigerate for a day or two, or freeze.

Note: When you bone the veal neck, be sure to save the bones for soups or stock.

Chicken and Chipolata

The Australians are not generally credited with creative cookery, but they did adapt the British oxtail soup to kangaroo tail and they stuffed a steak with oysters before grilling it, calling it carpetbag steak. In this creation, they stuff a roasting chicken with small whole French sausage. I adapted the recipe from *Australia the Beautiful Cookbook* by Elise Pasco and Cherry Ripe. Be sure to try it.

1 roasting chicken, about 4 pounds

about ¾ pound chipolata sausage links

1 Granny Smith apple

1 medium onion, chopped

1 to 2 tablespoons melted butter

1 teaspoon chopped fresh sage

salt and freshly ground black pepper, to taste

Preheat the oven to 350 degrees F. Peel, core, and chop the apple. Bring some water to a boil in a pot. Simmer the sausages for a few minutes, drain, and cool. Trim the fat away from the chicken but do not skin. Sprinkle the inside of the chicken with salt, freshly ground black pepper, and sage. Stuff the cavity loosely with 1 tablespoon of the chopped onion, ¼ of the chopped apple, and 4 or 5 of the sausages. Set the rest of the onion, apple, and sausage aside. Baste the chicken heavily with butter, then sprinkle with salt and pepper. Place the chicken on a baking pan and position it in the upper third of the preheated oven. Bake for 1 hour and 40 minutes. Add the rest of the sausage, apple, and onion to the pan. Bake for another 20 minutes, or until the bird is done. Turn off the oven and let the chicken coast for 10 minutes. Place the chicken on a heated serving platter along with the sausage, apple, and onion. Serve hot.

Duck Sausage

Duck is one of my very favorite meats. Any kind can be used in this sausage, but the small wild ducks, such as teal, are difficult to bone and don't yield much meat. For starters, it's best to use the larger domestic ducks. You'll need 5 or 6 pounds of meat. Skin the ducks. (Be sure to render the fat, saving the cracklings for bread or to sprinkle over potatoes or salads. Also, save the bony parts for soup or stock.)

2 large Long Island ducks

1½ pounds pork butt or shoulder

1½ pounds veal

1½ tablespoons salt

2 teaspoons Quatre Épices

1 teaspoon freshly ground black pepper

½ teaspoon dried marjoram

½ teaspoon dried sage

1½ cups cold water

hog casings

Skin the ducks and fillet the breast. Cut the breast meat into ¼- to ½-inch cubes; set aside. Bone the rest of the ducks and cut the meat into chunks for grinding. Cut the veal and pork into chunks. Spread the veal, pork, and duck chunks (but not the breast meat) onto your work surface. Sprinkle evenly with the salt and spices. Grind with a ⅛-inch plate, or twice with a ³⁄₁₆-inch plate. Mix the ground meat and diced duck breast. Stir in the cold water. Stuff into hog casings, tying off in 6-inch links. Cook or refrigerate immediately, or freeze. To cook, panfry the links in butter over low heat until done, or grill over a low charcoal or wood fire.

Crépinettes

This tasty sausage is made by wrapping seasoned sausage meat in caul fat, then frying the roll until crisp. Caul fat is the sheetlike membrane extending from the stomach over the intestines; it can be purchased in some meat stores, or might be available on special order. For making crépinettes, the sheet of fat should be soaked in warm water until it is pliable and then cut with kitchen shears into 4- to 6-inch squares or rectangles. Place a little sausage mix into each piece of caul fat, roll, and flatten slightly to about ½-inch thickness. (Some experts shape the meat into triangles, then wrap it accordingly, ending up with a sausage that resembles an arrowhead.) Fry until done. Enjoy.

Any good bulk sausage mix can be cooked by this method. If you want something special, try grinding 2 pounds of pork loin with 4 ounces of chopped truffles, all moistened with a good red wine.

Champagne Sausage

Here's an expensive sausage for special occasions. Be sure to sample the champagne while grinding the meat.

10 pounds pork butt or shoulder

1 dozen chicken eggs, whisked

12 ounces fresh mushrooms, finely chopped

2 bottles cold champagne

3 tablespoons Quatre Épices

1½ tablespoons salt

sheep casings

Cut the pork into chunks, spread them over your work surface, and sprinkle on the spice mix, salt, and chopped mushrooms. Grind the mix with a 1/8-inch plate (or grind twice with a 3/16-inch plate) then mix in the chicken eggs and champagne, saving a little champagne to sip while you stuff the meat into sheep casings, tying off every 6 inches or so. Bring some water to a boil in a large pot, insert the sausage, and simmer for 15 minutes. Sauté the sausage in butter.

Variation: If you really want to spend lots of money, reduce the mushrooms and make up the bulk with chopped truffles.

Saucisses de Toulouse

These plump sausages, made with chopped pork, are best stuffed into rather large hog casings.

10 pounds pork butt

4 tablespoons salt

4 tablespoons sugar

1 tablespoon Quatre Épices

1 to 2 cups water

large hog casings

Dice the meat and mix in the salt, sugar, and Quatre Épices. Place in a nonmetallic container, cover, and refrigerate overnight. Work in the water and stuff the mixture into hog casings, tying off in 6-inch links. Refrigerate for up to 2 days or freeze. To cook, simmer in water to make sure the pork is cooked through, then fry or grill. This sausage can also be used in soups and stews.

Herter's Soup Bourbon

After claiming that bourbon whiskey was made from grape seeds in France during the Middle Ages, George Leonard Herter, coauthor of *Bull Cook and Authentic Historical Recipes and Practices,* attributed this "authentic" soup to a cook employed by the Duke of Clermont. The Duke, Herter said, liked the soup so much that he ate it every Sunday, Tuesday, and Thursday. Being something of a fanatic about cauliflower as well as sausage, I was eager to test the recipe. But I couldn't in good conscience follow the directions. Herter starts off by boiling the cauliflower and celery for an hour before adding the sausage. This makes the cauliflower a little mushy, so I have cut back on the cooking times. Suit yourself.

¾ **pound pork sausage**

1 **medium head cauliflower**

5 **ribs celery with tops**

3 **tablespoons minced fresh parsley**

2 **green onions**

3 **chicken eggs**

salt and freshly ground pepper, to taste

Heat 3 quarts of water in a large pot. Break up the head of cauliflower, cutting it into 2-inch pieces. Cut the celery into ½-inch slices, and mince the leaves. Mince the parsley. Cut the green onions and tops into ¼-inch pieces. Cut the sausages into ½- or ¾-inch wheels. As soon as the water starts boiling, add all the chopped ingredients, salt, and pepper. Bring to a new boil, reduce the heat, cover, and simmer for 20 minutes. Whisk the eggs in a bowl with the aid of a fork. Then—here's the trick—add the eggs to the soup by dribbling them from the fork, then stirring them into the mixture, working with a small amount at a time. If all goes well, the egg will resemble noodles. Serve hot in soup bowls, along with buttered bread.

10

Scandinavian Sausages

The potato, which originated in the cool Andes region of South America, was not a big hit when the Spanish first took it to Europe. In fact, it became popular in Scandinavia long before it was generally accepted in many parts of the Continent. A major use of the potato was as an ingredient (possibly a filler) in sausages. Potato sausages are still popular, and all the Scandinavian countries have at least one favorite recipe, usually made with beef, pork, and potatoes, and pretty much the same sausages can be found in strong Swedish, Danish, Norwegian, and Finnish communities in the United States and Canada. Some of the recipes call for cooked potatoes, some for raw potatoes.

The Vikings, I might add, brought the sausage idea to Scandinavia from the warmer parts of Europe. Because of the Scandinavian climate, the highly spiced and hard sausages didn't take hold as deeply as the softer kinds. On the other hand, the hard air-dried sausage, such as the Göteborg, was ideal for taking along on lengthy sea voyages and consequently did not go unnoticed by the Vikings.

Potatis Korv

Here's a Swedish sausage made with cooked potatoes, pork, and beef. This recipe calls for only 4 pounds of meat, but note that it contains a large volume of potatoes.

2 pounds lean beef

2 pounds fatty pork (such as butt)

10 pounds potatoes (peeled weight)

2 large onions, chopped

10 cloves garlic, minced

2 tablespoons salt

1 tablespoon white pepper

½ tablespoon freshly ground black pepper

½ tablespoon ground allspice

½ teaspoon ground mace

½ teaspoon ground nutmeg

ham stock or chicken broth (or bouillon)

hog casings

Peel, dice, and boil the potatoes for about 10 minutes, or until they are done but not mushy. Cool and mash the potatoes, permitting a few small lumps. Cut the meat into chunks, mix in the onions, garlic, and spices, and grind with a ³⁄₁₆-inch plate. Mix the potatoes and ground meat. Stuff into hog casings, tying off in 12-inch links. Tie the ends of each link together, forming a ring. Heat some ham stock or chicken broth in a pot. Simmer the sausage for 45 minutes. Refrigerate. Serve hot or cold.

Norwegian Raw Potato Sausage

Here's an excellent sausage that is seasoned, except for salt and pepper, during cooking. Be sure to try it.

10 pounds pork butt or shoulder

5 pounds peeled potatoes

1 large onion

6 cups chicken broth

salt (used twice)
1 tablespoon white pepper
1 tablespoon allspice
3 bay leaves
hog casings

Dice the potatoes, meat, and onion. Mix on your work surface, sprinkling on the white pepper and 1 tablespoon of salt. Grind with a ³⁄₁₆-inch plate. Stuff into hog casings, tying off in 8-inch links. Sprinkle the links with salt and hang in a cool place overnight. To cook, bring the chicken broth to a boil, add the bay leaves, 1 teaspoon salt, and the allspice. Simmer the sausages for 1 hour. Serve hot.

Perunamakkara

According to *The Complete Sausage Cookbook* by Jack Sleight, this is the most popular of the Finnish homemade sausages. It is made with lean meats without the addition of animal fat.

7 pounds lean pork
3 pounds lean beef
4 large potatoes
8 cups milk
1 tablespoon salt, plus additional
1 tablespoon ground ginger
1 teaspoon ground nutmeg
hog casings

Peel, boil, cool, and mash the potatoes. Cut the meats into chunks, mix, and spread out over your work surface. Sprinkle evenly with 1 tablespoon salt, the ground ginger, and nutmeg. Grind the mix with a ³⁄₁₆-inch plate. Mix in the mashed potatoes and milk. Stuff loosely into hog casings, tying off in 6-inch links. Sprinkle the links with salt and refrigerate overnight. For longer storage, freeze or soak in a brine made with 3 tablespoons salt per quart of water.

To cook, simmer the sausages for 15 minutes, pricking them here and there to keep them from bursting. Serve hot.

Göteborg

This Swedish sausage, made of beef and pork, is stuffed into beef casings and air-dried.

6 pounds beef

4 pounds fatty pork butt (certified)

2 cups dry sherry

¾ cup salt

4 tablespoons ground mustard seed

4 tablespoons sugar

2 tablespoons crushed peppercorns

2 tablespoons minced fresh thyme

1 tablespoon ground cardamom

beef casings (middles)

Cut the meats into chunks suitable for grinding, sprinkle evenly with the salt, pack into a plastic tray, cover, and refrigerate for 48 hours. Spread the salty meats over your work surface, sprinkle with the spices and seasonings, and grind with a ³⁄₁₆-inch plate. Mix in the sherry and stuff into sewn beef middle casings. Stuff the sausages tightly, trying to avoid any air bubbles. Hang the sausages to dry for 4 or 5 hours. Cold-smoke for 12 hours, then dry in a cool airy place for 10 to 12 weeks, as discussed in Chapter 3.

To cook, simmer the sausage in stews and soups.

Medisterpølse

This Danish pork sausage is made with finely ground pork, stuffed into sheep casings. The recipe calls for beef stock, but it's okay to use canned broth or bouillon cubes with water.

10 pounds pork butt or shoulder

1 large onion, minced

3 tablespoons salt

1 tablespoon white pepper

1 teaspoon freshly ground black pepper

1 teaspoon ground cardamom

½ teaspoon ground allspice

½ teaspoon ground clove
2 cups beef stock
sheep casings

Cut the pork into chunks suitable for grinding, spread out on a work surface, sprinkle evenly with the onion and seasonings, grind with a ³⁄₁₆- or ¼-inch plate, and then grind twice more with a ⅛-inch plate. Work in the beef broth a little at a time. Stuff into sheep casings. To cook, fry or grill until well done, or simmer in broth for 10 minutes, then panfry. These can be refrigerated for a few days or frozen for longer storage.

Other European Sausages

S ausages are popular all over Europe, and many of the recipes are quite similar from one country to another. Indeed, the map of Europe—considering the dissolution of the Soviet Union and recent new lines drawn in the Balkans—tends to change faster than old cultural ties. Other recipes in remote regions are quite unique, as far as cookbooks go, and are not likely to have broad appeal for modern readers. On the island of Corsica, for example, one may find *tripa*—sheep casings stuffed with spinach, beets, herbs, and sheep's blood, cooked in salted water.

In any case, here are some European favorites to try, along with some classical recipes that call for sausage.

Kielbasa

The traditional Polish sausage, which is also popular in other European countries as well as in the United States, is called kielbasa. It is usually made with pork. Other meats can be added, but pork is the main ingredient. It is seasoned generously, and almost always contains garlic. The kielbasa sold in American markets is usually lightly smoked, but traditionally the sausage is consumed fresh. A middling-to-large sausage, it is sometimes stuffed in beef rounds. The larger hog casings will do. Kielbasa is about 12 inches long and 1½ inches in diameter. It is marketed in the shape of a horseshoe. The recipe below is rather basic.

10 pounds fatty fresh pork (butt will do), partly frozen

1 large onion, chopped

4 cloves garlic, minced

6 tablespoons salt

2 tablespoons Hungarian paprika

1 tablespoon coarsely ground black pepper

1 tablespoon red pepper flakes

1 teaspoon dried marjoram

2 cups ice water

beef casings or large hog casings

Cut the chilled or partly frozen meat into cubes. Spread the cubes out on your work surface, then sprinkle evenly with all the other ingredients except for the ice water. Grind the meat with a ³⁄₁₆-inch plate, mix in the ice water thoroughly with your hands, and stuff in large hog casings or small beef rounds, tying off in 12-inch or longer lengths. Dry the sausages overnight in a cool, airy place or in your refrigerator. These sausages are best when simmered for an hour or so, or used in stews such as bigos, a Polish national stew. They are also delicious when baked at 425 degrees F for 45 minutes, or when grilled slowly over charcoal.

These sausages can be cold-smoked for an hour or two for flavor, but they should not be considered cured. Note that most of the kielbasa sold in American supermarkets is lightly smoked and precooked.

Variations: Reduce the pork measure and add a little beef or veal. Also, vary the spices, adding, perhaps, a little allspice and summer savory.

🌭 Bigos

This old stew was originally made with bear, venison, boar, and other game. These days, pork and beef are used, along with spicy sausage to flavor the whole.

½ pound kielbasa, cut into 1-inch wheels
½ pound beef, cut into 1-inch cubes
½ pound pork, cut into 1-inch cubes
¼ pound salt pork, diced
2 pounds sauerkraut
1 large onion, chopped
8 to 12 ounces fresh mushrooms, sliced
2 cups beef broth
½ cup white wine
1 tablespoon Hungarian paprika
1 teaspoon freshly ground black pepper
2 bay leaves

Fry the salt pork until crisp in a large stove-top Dutch oven. Remove and drain the salt pork, leaving the drippings in the pot. Sauté the onion and mushrooms for 5 or 6 minutes. Brown the cubed pork and beef. Add the sausage, beef broth, wine, paprika, black pepper, and bay leaves. Bring to a boil, reduce the heat, cover, and simmer for 2 hours. Add the sauerkraut. Bring to a new boil, reduce the heat, and simmer for a few minutes. Serve hot, along with a hot crusty bread. Save the salt pork cracklings for salad or baked potatoes, or perhaps sprinkle them over each serving of bigos.

🌭 Hunter's Potatoes

Like bigos, this is an old hunter's dish, often made in camp. Leftovers are especially good, according to Jack Czarnecki, author of *Joe's Book of Mushroom Cookery,* from which this recipe has been adapted. Like many good camp dishes, exact measurements of ingredients aren't necessary. The dish is best cooked in a large pot. I use a cast-iron stove-top Dutch oven.

kielbasa, sliced

bacon strips

potatoes, sliced

carrots, sliced

fresh mushrooms, sliced

onions, sliced

a few cabbage leaves (red or white)

salt and freshly ground black pepper

Line the bottom of the pot with sliced bacon. Add a layer of potatoes, carrots, mushrooms, onions, and sausage, in that order. Sprinkle with a little salt and pepper. Repeat the layers until the pot is full. Cover the layers with cabbage leaves and a tight lid. Place on low heat. Cook for 1 hour, or, if you prefer, bake in a 350 degree F oven for 1 hour.

Buckwheat Sausages

Buckwheat sausage of one sort or another is made in Russia and several other parts of Europe. Sometimes the sausage is made with the aid of blood, and sometimes with liver, trotters, or snouts, along with various other ingredients. I have added a little beef broth to the recipe below, just in case the buckwheat turns out a little on the dry side. Whole buckwheat groats can be purchased from King Arthur Flour (see Sources, page 193) and possibly other outlets.

6 pounds fresh pork butt

4 pounds cooked buckwheat groats

3 tablespoons salt

2 tablespoons freshly ground black pepper

1 teaspoon ground dried marjoram

hog casings

Cook the buckwheat in water and set aside to cool. Cut the pork into chunks suitable for grinding, spread it over your work surface, and sprinkle evenly with the salt, pepper, and marjoram. Grind with a ¼- to ⅜-inch plate. Mix in 4 pounds of cooked buckwheat and some beef broth if needed. Stuff into hog casings. Cook by simmering the links in broth or by baking.

Smoked Hungarian Sausage

The fresh pork used in this recipe should be about 25 percent fat. If in doubt, separate the lean meat and fat, using 6 pounds lean and 2 pounds fat.

8 pounds fresh Boston butt or picnic ham (certified)
2 pounds lean beef
¼ cup minced or crushed fresh garlic
¼ cup Hungarian paprika, sweet or mild
¼ cup salt
1 tablespoon freshly ground black pepper
2 teaspoons Prague Powder 1 (optional; see Chapter 3)
½ teaspoon ground clove
hog casings

Trim the meat, cut it into chunks, and spread out on your work surface, mixing it more or less equally. Sprinkle on the garlic. Thoroughly mix the salt, pepper, paprika, Prague Powder, and clove; sprinkle the mix evenly on the meat.

Grind the meat using a ¼- or ⅜-inch wheel. Stuff into hog casings, tying off in convenient lengths. Cold-smoke the meat for several hours at a temperature of less than 90 degrees F. Or, if you have a small commercial unit, smoke it at 150 degrees F or so for about an hour. If in doubt about the temperature, use a thermometer. (It's best to avoid the temperate range between 90 and 150 degrees F.) Air-dry the sausage in a cool, airy place for 2 days. Cook thoroughly before eating, remembering to punch a few holes in the casing. I like to cook these in a little oil in an electric skillet, tightly covered, so that the cooking process is a combination of frying and steaming.

The sausage will keep for several days in the refrigerator. Freeze for longer storage.

Hurka

In addition to paprikash recipes, the Hungarians also make an excellent sausage with cooked pork and rice.

5 pounds cooked rice

5 pounds fatty pork (Boston butt or shoulder will do)

2 pounds pork heart

2 pounds pork jowl

1 pound pork liver

2 medium-to-large onions

⅓ cup salt

1½ tablespoons freshly ground black pepper

¼ teaspoon ground dried marjoram

lard

boiling water

medium hog casings

Cut the meats into chunks suitable for grinding, keeping the liver separate. Put the pork, jowl, and heart into a pot, cover with water, bring to a boil, reduce the heat, and simmer for 30 or 40 minutes. Add the liver during the last 10 minutes. Drain, saving the stock. Chop and sauté the onions in a little lard. Spread the drained meats out on your work surface, mixing evenly. Sprinkle evenly with the salt, pepper, marjoram, and sautéed onions. Grind the meats with a ³⁄₁₆-inch plate. Using your hands, mix with the cooked rice and 1 cup of the stock from the boiled meats. Stuff into medium hog casings. Drop the links into boiling water for 1 to 2 minutes. Dry and refrigerate until needed. Freeze for long storage.

Variations: Omit the liver if you prefer. If you like the liver, however, try a mix of 4 pounds butt, 2 pounds liver, 2 pounds lights (lungs), and 2 pounds heart. Also, use beef heart instead of pork if it is more readily available, and substitute pork belly for jowls if it is more convenient.

Yugoslavian Blood Sausage

Several Yugoslavian sausage recipes call for pig's blood, along with the head, heart, lungs (or lights), and a pork butt. Unless you butcher your own hogs, it may be difficult to obtain all the ingredients. Here's a recipe, adapted from *The Sausage-Making Cookbook* by Jerry Predika, that is more easily managed. I find it interesting because it makes use of barley, one of my favorite groats.

4 pounds cooked pork butt

2 quarts fresh pork blood

1½ cups dried pearl barley

1 cup sugar

2 teaspoons vinegar

1 teaspoon ground ginger

1 teaspoon ground allspice

2 tablespoons salt

hog casings

Soak the barley overnight in water. Cut the pork butt into chunks, cover with water, and simmer for 30 minutes. Drain and refrigerate the pork. Put 3 cups of the broth into a pot, bring to a boil, and add the barley. Simmer, covered, for 15 minutes. Add a little water if needed and simmer for another 5 minutes. Stir the vinegar into the pork blood. Grind the cooked pork with a ³⁄₁₆-inch plate. Mix in the other ingredients. Stuff into hog casings. Simmer the sausage for 15 minutes. Serve warm or chilled. Refrigerate for several days, or freeze for longer storage.

Note: For other interesting recipes for Yugoslavian blood sausages, see *The Sausage-Making Cookbook.*

Lithuanian Sausage

Here's an easy sausage recipe from Lithuania. Although heavy on onion, it is rather mild—and very good.

10 pounds pork butt

2 pounds minced onion

5 cups salt

1 tablespoon coarse black pepper

1 tablespoon ground allspice

medium hog casings

Trim a little fat from the meat and heat it in a skillet until you fry out a little oil. Sauté the onion for a few minutes, until it turns transparent. Set aside. Cut the meat into chunks and sprinkle it with salt, pepper, and allspice. Grind with a ³⁄₁₆-inch plate. Mix in the cooked onion and any grease from the skillet. Stuff into medium hog casings, twisting into 5-inch connected lengths. Let dry to the touch. Heat some salted water in a large pot. Simmer (do not boil) the sausage links for about 20 minutes. Dry and refrigerate or freeze. To prepare for the table, brown the links nicely in a little oil or butter in a skillet.

Mititei (Romanian)

Romanian sausages, of which there are several, tend to have some pleasant surprises in the ingredient list, such as dill seeds and lovage. Here's an all-beef recipe calling for baking soda, olive oil, and lots of parsley.

10 pounds beef (such as chuck roast)

2 cups water

1½ cups olive oil

¾ cup dried parsley

15 cloves garlic, minced

3 tablespoons salt

2 tablespoons baking soda

2 tablespoons freshly ground black pepper

Cut the beef into chunks suitable for grinding, mix in the dry seasonings, and grind with a ³⁄₁₆-inch plate. Mix in the garlic, water, and olive oil. Stuff into hog casings. Dry and cook, refrigerate for a few days, or freeze. To cook, grill over charcoal, bake, or broil.

Bulgarian Veal or Lamb Sausages

I've seen several recipes for Bulgarian sausages and all of them had one thing in common: a short list of ingredients. Here's one that is made from either beef or lamb. I tried it a couple of times, with great success, but I used 1 pound of meat (instead of 10) because I didn't want to store excess sausage that contained uncooked chicken eggs.

1 pound veal or lamb
1 medium onion, minced
1 large chicken egg
½ teaspoon salt
¼ teaspoon freshly ground black pepper

Cut the meat into chunks, then grind it twice with a ⅛- or 3/16-inch plate. Mix in the other ingredients. Take out small portions with a tablespoon measure and roll into small sausages about 2 inches long. Fry, broil, or grill over charcoal. These require careful handling.

Hot-Smoked Swiss Sausage

Switzerland enjoys a number of sausages, mostly variations on German, French, and Italian themes, depending on the region and its influences. If there is a truly national Swiss sausage, it would probably be a farmer's recipe making good use of milk or cream, as in the following recipe, or some other dairy product. Because this sausage is hot-smoked, it's a good choice for backyard chefs. Note, however, that this sausage is very mild, which is typical of sausages from cold lands. Add a tablespoon of freshly ground black pepper if you long for it.

6 pounds beef chuck
4 pounds pork butt
3 cups heavy cream
1 cup cold water
4 tablespoons salt, plus additional
2 tablespoons caraway seed
1 tablespoon ground allspice
brown sugar, to taste
medium hog casings

Cut the beef and pork into chunks suitable for grinding, spread the chunks out on your work surface, and sprinkle evenly with the salt, caraway seed, and allspice. Grind with a ³⁄₁₆-inch plate, then grind again with a ⅛-inch plate. Mix in the cream and water. Stuff into medium hog casings, tying off in 6-inch connected links. Sprinkle with salt and brown sugar. Refrigerate overnight. Also soak some hardwood chips in water. When you are ready to cook, build a charcoal fire on one side of a large grill. Place some wood chips on the fire. Hot-smoke the sausages for about 3 hours, or until done. (The lower the temperature, the longer the cooking time and the greater the smoke. Much depends on your fire, grill, draft settings, and so on.) If in doubt, check the internal temperature of the sausage before serving, making sure it is at least 150 degrees F. This sausage can also be baked slowly in the oven.

12

Middle Eastern and African Sausages

The vast area represented by the title of this chapter might suggest a long text, but the facts indicate that the sausage has not been very important in the culinary and cultural history of these lands. Indeed, we have to go all the way to South Africa to find a widespread passion for sausage, and even here the influence is probably more European (primarily Dutch) than African.

In the Middle East, the hog is not a very popular meat, owing mostly to religious and cultural traditions, and to the fact that the countryside is more suited to goats and sheep than to pigs. The region doesn't have the vast oak and beech forests that helped make the pig popular in Europe and, early on, in North America. Also, the Jews, Muslims, and Hindus forbid the use of pork in any form, and there may be some resistance to blood and to the idea of stuffing meat into intestines. On the other hand, ground meat is very popular in the Middle East and North Africa. It is often shaped around flat skewers, and is sometimes made into little sausage shapes. Grilling over charcoal is a very popular way of cooking the meat, usually lamb, if we may trust modern Americanized cookbooks, but perhaps camel, goat, antelope, and other good meats. These ground meat fingers are very close to sausage without the casing, so I have included such a recipe from Algeria.

Lebanon bologna, I might explain before proceeding, is an American product, having been developed in Lebanon, Pennsylvania, and as such, does not appear in this chapter.

Algerian Casbah Sausages

Here's an excellent Algerian recipe for a sausage-shaped meat, adapted from *The Grains Cookbook* by Bert Greene.

1 pound ground lamb

½ pound ground veal

½ cup quick rolled oats

¼ cup butter

1 medium-to-large onion, finely chopped

1 clove garlic, finely chopped

2 tablespoons finely chopped fresh parsley

2 tablespoons water

1 tablespoon fresh lemon juice

1 tablespoon olive oil

1 chicken egg, whisked

¼ teaspoon ground cinnamon

⅛ teaspoon ground allspice

hot pepper sauce, to taste

salt and pepper, to taste

Grind the meats with a ³⁄₁₆-inch plate. Heat the olive oil and about half the butter in a skillet, then sauté the onion and garlic for 4 or 5 minutes. Set aside. In a large bowl, mix the meats, oats, and egg. Add the sautéed onion and garlic, allspice, cinnamon, parsley, lemon juice, water, salt, pepper, and a little hot pepper sauce to taste. Mix thoroughly with your hands and shape into small sausage shapes. Heat the rest of the butter in the skillet. Add 5 or 6 of the sausages.

Cook over medium heat until browned on all sides, which should take about 8 minutes for each batch. Serve hot.

Armenian Lamb Sausage

Here's an unusual sausage made of ground lamb and heavily flavored with fresh mint. Any good cut of lamb can be used. Try shoulder, which is usually available at meat shops. Be sure to make a lamb stew with the bones.

10 pounds boned lamb meat

2 cups finely chopped onion

1½ cups chopped fresh mint

2 cups water

15 to 20 cloves garlic, minced

3 tablespoons salt

1½ tablespoons freshly ground black pepper

sheep casings

Cut the meat into chunks, spread them out on your work surface, sprinkle with salt and black pepper, and grind with a ³⁄₁₆- or ⅛-inch plate. With your hands mix in the onion, garlic, mint, and water. Stuff the mixture into sheep casings. These fresh sausages will keep in the refrigerator for several days, or they can be frozen for longer storage. To cook, grill over charcoal or broil in the oven. Try cutting them into chunks and grilling them on a skewer, along with suitable kabob vegetables; serve on rice.

Moroccan Lamb Sausage

The North Africans make a lamb sausage similar to the Armenian recipe above. In this Moroccan recipe, fresh chopped parsley takes the place of mint and, predictably, more spices are added.

10 pounds boned lamb meat

3 cups finely chopped onion

3 cups finely chopped parsley

2 cups water

3 tablespoons salt

1 to 2 tablespoons cayenne

1 tablespoon freshly ground black pepper

1 tablespoon dried oregano

1 tablespoon dried coriander

1 tablespoon dried marjoram

1 teaspoon crushed cumin seed

sheep casings

Cut the meat into chunks, spread them out on your work surface, sprinkle evenly with the dry spices, and grind with a ⅛- or ³⁄₁₆-inch plate. With your hands mix in the onion, parsley, and water. Stuff the mixture into sheep casings. To cook, grill or broil. These sausages will keep for several days in the refrigerator, or they can be frozen for longer storage.

Greek Sausage

Although sausage was mentioned in both the *Iliad* and the *Odyssey*, as well in other ancient writings, neither ancient nor modern Greece has left us a sausage of worldwide renown. I have read that the sausage originated in Greece, but this claim is difficult to prove. Who knows? The Greeks were very important in the history of the sausage, however, for they influenced the Silesians and Romans. Although several sausages are made in modern Greece, most of these are similar to European sausages. One exception, it seems to me, is the following, which uses orange zest.

10 pounds pork butt

2 cups red wine

15 cloves garlic, minced

4 tablespoons salt

3 tablespoons freshly grated orange zest

2 tablespoons dried coriander

1 tablespoon dried thyme

1 tablespoon dried marjoram

2 crushed bay leaves

hog casings

Cut the pork into chunks suitable for grinding. Spread these out on your work surface, sprinkle evenly with the salt and dry ingredients, and grind with a ³⁄₁₆-inch plate. Mix in the wine, orange peel, and garlic. Stuff into hog casings or shape into patties. Cook immediately, refrigerate for 2 days, or freeze. To cook, poach the sausage in a little simmering water for 10 minutes, dry, and grill or fry. These sausages can also be used in soups, stews, and casseroles. Try some in bulk form in a batch of Greek-style moussaka.

Boerish Sausage

Outdoor grilling is very popular in South Africa, where the cookout is known as *braai*. These events call for freshly baked bread, sosaties, and large round sausage called boerewors. The sosaties, of course, are lamb kabobs marinated with curry and other spices; the dish is of Malay origin, brought to southern Africa by Malaysian slaves of the Dutch settlers. The boerewors are of Dutch origin (possibly adapted for local South African meats such as aardvark). The bacon used in the recipe can, of course, be bacon ends and pieces, which are usually available at bargain prices.

6 pounds lean beef

2 pounds pork shoulder

2 pounds bacon

2 cups vinegar

3 tablespoons ground coriander

3 tablespoons salt

1 teaspoon freshly ground black pepper

1 teaspoon ground nutmeg

1 teaspoon ground clove

hog casings

Cut the meats and bacon into chunks, mix, and spread out on a work surface. Sprinkle evenly with the dry spices. Grind with a ¼- to ⅓-inch plate. Mix in the vinegar and refrigerate for 3 hours. Regrind with a ⅛-inch plate. Stuff into hog casings, tying off into 4-

to 5-inch connected links. To cook, grill over charcoal or wood coals. Boerewors can also be baked in an oven or simmered for a few minutes in water or broth, then fried in a skillet.

Asian Sausages

Although the pig was first domesticated in China, the variety of sausages in that part of the world doesn't even begin to rival that of northern Europe. Typically, the Chinese sausage—called *lop chiang*—is hard, dry, strong, and on the sweet side. By contrast, the Thai like their sausage hot and spicy. The rest of Asia doesn't cook much sausage, and the island nations lean toward cooking the pig whole. Indonesians love pork sausages, but for the most part these are made by recipes brought to the islands from Europe.

Basic Chinese Sausage

Although the Chinese market a dried sausage made with only pork, pork fat, salt, and sugar, I consider soy sauce and rice wine to be essential to the real thing. Here's a standard recipe.

10 pounds fatty fresh pork
2 cups soy sauce
2 cups rice wine
½ cup sugar

½ cup salt
hog casings

Grind the meat with a ³⁄₁₆-inch plate. Mix in the rest of the ingredients and refrigerate for 2 days. Stuff the mixture into hog casings, tie off in 6-inch links, and dry in a cool, airy place for about 8 weeks. The links can also be cold-smoked for part of the curing period. After the drying period, I prefer to wrap them in plastic film and refrigerate or freeze them until needed. Being dry and hard, these sausages are best when steamed or simmered in stock, or used in various recipes. Typically, they are sliced diagonally before serving.

Variations: Note that the basic recipe doesn't contain any pepper. If you expect hot stuff in your sausage, try the Szechwan variety, made by adding ¼ cup crushed red pepper flakes and 1 tablespoon ground ginger to the above measures, along with 15 or 20 minced cloves of garlic. Cut the sugar measure in half.

✐ Hacked Chicken and Chinese Sausage

The Chinese sometimes cut a chicken into chunks, bones and all, before cooking it. It's a true hack job, like Kentucky Fried Chicken, but remember that the bones add to the flavor. To hack a bird, first disjoint it and then chop it into bite-size pieces with the aid of a meat cleaver. (If you prefer, first bone the chicken and then cut it into pieces with a regular knife. Then hack the bones and add them to the pot with the chicken.) For best results, use a barnyard or free-range chicken, plucked instead of skinned. If you use supermarket chicken with lots of fat, skin it. The recipe calls for dried Chinese forest mushrooms. These are available in Asian markets. They are very flavorful, but they are a little expensive. If you have dried morels or other dried mushrooms, use them.

1 chicken, about 3 pounds, cut into chunks
1 pound Chinese sausage, cut into chunks
1 ounce dried Chinese forest mushrooms
2 tablespoons soy sauce
1 tablespoon rice wine, dry sherry, or vermouth
1 tablespoon cornstarch

Soak the mushrooms in water for several hours, or overnight, then slice and drain them. Save the soaking liquid. Chop the chicken into chunks. Marinate the the chicken, sausage, and sliced mushrooms for 2 or 3 hours in a nonmetallic container with a mixture of the soy sauce, wine, and cornstarch, along with 2 tablespoons of the liquid in which the mushrooms were soaked. Drain the chicken, discarding the marinade liquid.

Rig for steaming. If you don't have a steamer, pour a little water into a pot or wok, fit with a rack (which should be above the water level), and bring to a boil. Place the pieces of chicken onto the rack, cover with the sausage and mushrooms, and steam for about 45 minutes, or until the chicken is tender. Serve hot, along with rice, Chinese vegetables, and condiments of your choice, plus, perhaps, a dipping sauce.

♪ Chinese Pilau

Rice and sausage go together nicely, and the Chinese (before mechanical refrigeration became common) even stored dried sausages in the rice crock. They have an easy way of flavoring rice with sausage. Simply cook the rice as usual, but place some links of sausage on top. (There are many ways of cooking rice, but, for this recipe, I use the more or less standard 2 cups of water for each 1 cup of rice, simmered without peeking for 20 minutes.) Be sure to prick the sausage links so that the juice will run down into the rice. When done, cut the sausages into thin slices and serve them along with the rice. Many peasant families serve only the sausage and rice for a meal, but, of course, they add steamed vegetables and other dishes for company.

Note that any good sausage can be cooked with rice by this method. If you don't have Chinese fare at hand, try dried chorizo for a Spanish touch or a pepperoni for Italian.

♪ Steamed Chinese Sausages and Chicken Eggs

Sausages and chicken eggs go together nicely in most lands. The Chinese, however, are more likely to use duck eggs. Because duck eggs aren't readily available in most American markets, I have substituted chicken eggs in the ingredients. If you've got fresh duck eggs, use four instead of six.

½ pound Chinese sausage, thinly sliced

½ pound fresh pork, chopped into ½-inch pieces

6 chicken eggs, whisked

1 small-to-medium onion, minced

2 green onions, minced with part of the green tops

½ cup chicken or duck stock

2 tablespoons light soy sauce

1 tablespoon peanut oil

1 teaspoon sugar

salt, to taste

Rig for steaming and heat the water to a boil. Mix all the ingredients in a bowl of suitable size, which should allow at least 1 inch of space at the top for expansion. Carefully place the bowl on a rack in the steamer pot or wok. Cover tightly. Steam on medium-low heat for about 45 minutes. Serve hot. Conveniently, this dish can be cooked ahead of time, cooled, and resteamed.

Spicy Thai Sausages

The Thai love sausages and have several sorts, all highly spiced. This version, adapted from the book *True Thai* by Victor Sodsook, is one of my favorite sausages because I love fish sauce. Although I have mixed feelings about most commercial curry powder, I do use canned red curry paste in this recipe. Sticklers for true Thai will choose to make their own curry paste.

The recipe also calls for fresh Kaffir lime leaves. If these are not available (fresh), substitute freshly grated lime zest. The fresh leaves are better, however, partly because they contribute green flecks to the sausages, as do the cilantro stems. (If you grow your own cilantro, as I do, you can also use some of the roots in this recipe. Also, the seeds of the cilantro plant, when ground, are the same as coriander.)

My version of the recipe also calls for only 1 pound of fatty meat (I usually use pork butt or shoulder) whereas *True Thai,* I should point out, specified ¾ pound loin or tenderloin, which is very dry. Suit yourself. In either case, it's best to make a small batch of this sausage. Then, if you like the flavor, you can easily make a 10-pound batch simply by increasing the measures tenfold.

1 pound fatty pork
12 fresh Kaffir lime leaves or ½ teaspoon fresh lime zest
1 tablespoon Thai fish sauce
½ cup chopped fresh garlic
¼ cup finely chopped cilantro stems
1 tablespoon white pepper
½ to 1 tablespoon canned red curry paste
½ teaspoon crushed or ground coriander
hog casings

Cut the meat into chunks and mix in the Kaffir lime leaves, garlic, cilantro stems, white pepper, coriander, curry paste, and fish sauce. Grind the mixture with a ³⁄₁₆-inch plate. Mix again with your hands, then stuff it into medium hog casings, tying off every 4 inches. Refrigerate the links in a covered nonmetallic container overnight. Cook as needed, or freeze for longer storage.

Although these are rather spicy sausages, the Thai often serve them as an entree, along with suitable condiments, instead of using them to season other dishes in the Chinese manner. See the next two recipes.

Bangkok Fry

The method of cooking these sausages is nothing new to connoisseurs, but the manner of serving is likely to be unusual to culinary sports of the Western world. Having been raised on a peanut farm, I was especially interested in the recipe. (The Thai, by the way, are one of the few peoples who enjoy boiled green peanuts. I used to sell these around our town when I was a boy.)

Thai sausages
small lettuce or salad greens

cucumber, peeled, seeded, and sliced
chopped cilantro
fresh gingerroot, sliced very thinly
chili peppers, chopped and well-seeded
1 lemon
chopped peanuts
peanut oil

Prepare the condiments first, arranging them (unmixed) as you go on a serving platter. Cut off the ends of the lemon but do not peel it. Slice it into ½-inch wheels, then dice them. Seed and chop the chili peppers. Chop the cilantro. Chop the peanuts. Peel, seed, and slice the cucumber. Peel the gingerroot, then slice it very, very thinly. Select some small cup-shaped leaves of lettuce or other suitable salad greens. When the condiment platter is ready, quickly heat about 2 tablespoons of peanut oil in a heavy skillet. Cut the sausages into separate links, prick the links with a fork, and sauté them until nicely browned and cooked through, turning frequently. This should take about 10 minutes. Drain the sausages, cut them into 1-inch wheels, arrange them on a serving platter, and serve them with the condiments.

Each piece of sausage and a selection of condiments are wrapped in a lettuce leaf and eaten by hand, giving each diner a choice. This method permits me to pass on the cucumber, which doesn't agree with me, and will permit guests to vary the amount of chili or ginger. Serve with Thai beer.

♪ Grilled Thai Sausage

Build a charcoal fire. Grill the sausage links slowly, turning from time to time, until they are nicely browned and cooked through. Cut the grilled sausages into 1-inch wheels, then serve with Thai condiments, as discussed in the previous recipe.

Add some wood chips to the fire if you want some smoke. The Thai sometimes sprinkle the fire with dried coconut meat (left over from making coconut milk) to sweeten the smoke. They also wrap the sausage in banana leaves before grilling.

14

American and Canadian Sausages

I've seen hundreds of recipes for American and Canadian sausages, but the truth is that we are a nation of immigrant sausages. Not counting numerous local favorites and some brand names, only one American sausage has made a name for itself—Lebanon bologna. The real contribution that the New World made to sausage was the hot chili pepper. Another contribution (for better or worse) was even more basic, having to do with the nature of the meat.

Let me explain. In North America, the settlers found the hog to be highly adaptable, and, of course, the hog was easy for homesteaders to butcher as compared with beef. The hog quickly became by far the main meat in North America and remained so until a network of railroads was built to haul cattle from western ranches to eastern markets.

At first, hogs were allowed to roam free in almost all areas. At homesteads on the barrier islands of North Carolina, for example, the inhabitants fenced in the houses and turned the hogs loose, usually with various notches cut in the ear for identification. Trained dogs were used to round up and catch the hogs in the fall of the year. One problem was that acorns usually made up a large part of the diet at that time of the year, and many of the American oaks produce very bitter acorns as compared with European species. (There are exceptions, such as the white oak and live oak, which produce acorns with sweet meat and lots of usable oil.) The American acorns tended to cause the meat from the hogs to be bitter. So, the American settlers started penning up the hogs to fatten them for the slaughter. The pen, of course, also kept the hogs away from the acorns.

In Virginia, peanuts were used to fatten the hogs, and even today the famous Smithfield hams are made from hogs fattened on peanuts. As stated in the last chapter, I was born and raised on a peanut farm, so the idea has long been with me. At least in my neck of the woods, an entire peanut field (sometimes hundreds of acres) was fenced in and the hogs were loosed on it, free to root the nuts out of the ground. More likely, the peanuts were harvested and then the hogs were turned loose in the field to eat the nuts that were lost during the harvest. Corn was also "hogged off" in the same way, and I've known farmers to plant soybeans (runners) in corn just for forage. A few people even planted fields of chufas to fatten their hogs.

Also, many households in towns and country made use of just about anything edible, such as parsley and pigweeds, to feed a few pigs. In the Ozarks, an edible oak gall was fed to the hogs, along with table scraps. Slopping the hogs in troughs was an everyday household chore in some cases. Where I grew up, even cane skimmings (top scum and dredgings left from boiling cane juice down to syrup) were used to feed the hogs. Sometimes this stuff fermented, making the pigs tipsy.

I want to emphasize that hogs weren't only farm animals. Many small-town homes had a pigpen—and hogs were raised even in the cities. New York, I understand, permitted street hogs until well into the nineteenth century. The hogs helped control the garbage, just as they had done for centuries in European cities such as Rome and Paris. When a law forbidding the practice was passed in New York, the housewives, if we may believe food historian Waverley Root, armed themselves with broomsticks to fight off the hog carts. Of course, all the great cities of Europe used the hog as a garbage disposal.

In any case, the great American no-name sausage—made with thousands of variations—took place at the homestead. Most of these sausages were made of fatty scraps of meat at hog-killing time. While these sausages are very good and practical, some producers began to take pride in using whole shoulders and hams in their sausages instead of mere scraps. Some connoisseurs made what came to be known as whole-hog sausage.

But as a rule the home sausage was kept on the simple side. Salt, black pepper, sage, and red pepper flakes were often the only seasonings used. I can tell you from personal experience that hog-killing time—usually at first frost in the fall of the year—was special in many areas, and these simple sausages were the best of all. Some of these recipes were set forth in Chapter 1, but it would be impossible to cover them all.

To back up a little: Penning up the hogs so that they couldn't eat bitter acorns resulted in a fatter pig. This wasn't a bad trait at the time since lard was a very, very important cooking medium. From a purely culinary viewpoint, lard is still very good for cooking purposes. During my boyhood, lard was still very important, and at our house we had several five-gallon containers called lard cans. These days, of course, any animal fat is frowned upon by health experts and we are seeing a trend toward leaner and leaner pigs.

In addition to the typical North American household sausages, many communities made sausages from Old World recipes. In addition, ethnic communities (such as Chinatown) in various cities, often seaports, made traditional sausages, changing the recipes a little over a period of time. One other New World influence on sausages developed around French and Mexican sausages, modifying the recipes and also developing distinctive dishes making use of these sausages as an ingredient. Gumbo and menudo, for example. These traditions and recipes were covered in earlier chapters.

Lebanon Bologna

This all-beef bologna has a distinctive sour flavor that is hard to duplicate at home because it, like a true Smithfield ham, goes through a highly controlled environmental process. One of the Lebanon bologna recipes I have seen calls for Prague Powder 2, corn syrup solids, powdered dextrose, and Fermento. After being salted and cured for 5 to 6 days at 38 to 40 degrees F, it is mixed with spices and the additives, stuffed into large "protein-lined" casings, and hung to dry in three stages: 16 hours at 90 degrees F with 90 percent humidity; 28 hours at 105 degrees F with 85 percent humidity; and 6 hours at 110 degrees F with 85 percent humidity. The sausage is said to develop its tangy flavor during this 50 hours of curing. It can then be heavily smoked for a day or two. For a fully cooked product, the smokehouse temperature is increased to 150 degrees F. The sausage is then smoked until the internal temperature reaches 137 degrees F. It is then removed from the smokehouse and allowed to cool down to 110 degrees F. Finally, it is placed in a cooler and aged for 4 or 5 days.

I haven't tested the recipe because I don't have the facilities to control the temperature and humidity.

If you want to go the whole nine yards, check into Rytek Kutas's book *Great Sausage Recipes and Meat Curing*. Kutas will even sell you the Prague Powder and additives, along with environmental control machines and measuring devices. Good luck.

Meanwhile, you may want to hazard the following:

10 pounds lean beef

2 ounces salt

2 ounces sugar

1 tablespoon white pepper

1 tablespoon Hungarian paprika

¼ teaspoon sodium nitrite

¼ teaspoon sodium nitrate

1 teaspoon dried mustard

1 teaspoon ground ginger

½ teaspoon ground mace

large casings (5-inch diameter)

Cut the beef into ½- to ¾-inch chunks and place them in a large plastic tray. Mix a cure by combining the salt, sugar, and sodium nitrite. Sprinkle the cure evenly over the beef, tossing to coat all sides. Cover the tray and refrigerate for 8 days at about 35 degrees F. Remove the tray and mix in the other ingredients. Grind with a ³⁄₁₆-inch plate. Regrind, preferably with a ⅛-inch plate. Stuff into the casings. Hang and cold-smoke for 5 or 6 days. After smoking, hang the links in the refrigerator until needed. For extended storage, you may prefer to freeze the links.

Farm Sausage

As stated earlier, the great American sausage is a product of hog-killing time, and is made from fatty scraps accumulated during the butchering process. These sausages are very good, although they are a little on the fatty side and tend to shrink up when cooked. If you don't have a fat pig to kill, the mix can be approximated by using 8 or 9 parts fatty pork butt or shoulder mixed with 1 or 2 parts pure fat, as from fresh fatback. Since the pork butt or shoulder is about 30 percent fat, the result is a sausage that is about half fat. Some country recipes call for red pepper flakes, and some don't. I like to use lots of mild red pepper flakes, but be warned that some commercial red pepper is very hot and some is not. The sage is also optional, but I recommend it.

8 pounds pork butt

2 pounds fatback or other pork fat

5 tablespoons salt

1 tablespoon coarsely ground black pepper

1 tablespoon red pepper flakes (optional)

½ tablespoon dried minced sage (optional)

hog casings

Cut the pork and fat into chunks suitable for grinding. Mix and spread the chunks out on your work surface. Combine all the seasonings, then sprinkle evenly over the meat. Grind a little of the meat in a ³⁄₁₆- or ⅛-inch plate. Shape a patty and fry it in a skillet.

Taste and adjust the seasonings if required. Grind the meat and stuff into hog casings.

To cook these fresh pork sausages, simmer the links in a little water, covered tightly, for about 15 minutes. Dry the links with paper towels and fry them in a skillet until nicely browned. Many people will prefer the sausage merely fried, omitting the simmering. This sausage can also be used in recipes.

Tom Baxter's Best

Mr. Tom Baxter, an old friend of my father's, managed some farms owned by a Ford tractor dealer at a time when small tractors were replacing mules and workhorses. The dealer, who also had other business interests as well as culinary yearnings, traveled frequently and sometimes took Mr. Tom with him for company and to help with the driving. Toward the end of his days, Mr. Tom was recounting his culinary experiences one day, describing the menus in fancy restaurants from New Orleans to New York. But the best thing he had ever eaten, he said, his mouth watering, was homemade sausage, biscuits, and syrup. He was talking about locally made cane syrup. His sausage, as I remember it, was hot with red pepper flakes. I, too, have eaten, albeit infrequently, in New Orleans and New York, and, for brute flavor, I'll have to agree with Mr. Tom.

Deli Fare and Cold Cuts

B e warned that the recipes in this chapter yield sausages and sandwich meats that are different from their modern supermarket counterparts. Most of the commercial franks, for example, have a spongy texture and a slick surface, and contain lots of emulsified fat. The recipes herein yield a firmer and more flavorful sausage or sandwich meat. The casings of the homemade kinds, however, along with the firmer stuffings, do make the sausages a little tougher. Or different. You may be able to make a closer approximation of the commercial fare by zapping the meat in a high-speed food processor, as explained in Chapter 1; but remember that consistent results are difficult to achieve with home equipment. Besides, who wants to know how to do the wrong thing?

Frankfurter

Also known as hot dogs, wieners, wienerwurst, and franks, this is perhaps the world's most widely known sausage. Homemade hot dogs are so different from those sold in our supermarkets that we have to question the name. Countless recipes exist for franks, sometimes with a different ratio of beef to pork and always with a different set of spices. Try mine, below, then experiment.

6 pounds pork butt or shoulder

4 pounds beef

8 cloves garlic, minced

4 tablespoons salt

1½ tablespoons white pepper

1 tablespoon Hungarian paprika

1 tablespoon ground coriander

2 teaspoons ground mace

3 cups water

sheep casings

Cut the meat into chunks suitable for grinding, mix, and spread them over your work surface. Sprinkle evenly with the seasonings and garlic. Grind with a ³⁄₁₆-inch plate, then grind again with a ⅛-inch plate. Mix in the water and stuff into sheep casings, tying off in 6-inch lengths. Simmer them in hot water—do not boil, lest the links burst open—for 15 minutes or so, or until they float. Fat franks may require a longer simmering time before they float. Pat the franks dry with paper toweling and refrigerate or freeze until needed. Although cooked, these are usually heated before making hot dogs, or they are reheated or cooked in another recipe.

Smoked Frankfurters: Proceed as above until the links have been stuffed. Air-dry, then cold-smoke (at 120 degrees F or less) for about 2 hours, using any good hardwood. After smoking, proceed with the simmering.

✐ Hot Dogs

The essential ingredients for hot dogs include the bun, the dog, and condiments such as mustard and toppings such as chopped onion or sauerkraut. These are very good when made with simmered franks, but they can be improved simply by grilling or broiling.

If you use a plain steamed or boiled frank, it's best to have a soft bun, preferably steamed, and add a chili meat sauce (made with finely ground pork) and chopped onions.

Wiener Roast and Grilled Dogs

Build a charcoal or wood fire and let it burn down to coals, or rake some coals aside from the main fire. Stick a dog onto the end of a skewer or pointed stick and hold it over the coals, turning as needed, until it is nicely browned or perhaps charred. Place it into a fresh hot-dog bun and, using the bun for a grip, pull it off the stick. Spread on a little mayonnaise, catsup, and mustard. Chopped onion, pickle relish, and other go-withs help, but if you are cooking around a campfire it's best to keep things simple.

On the patio, the hot dogs can be grilled, in which case skewering isn't necessary for turning and handling. Use tongs.

In the kitchen, the hot dogs can be cooked on a stove-top grill and served at the table, along with a wide choice of condiments and go-withs.

Good Ol' Boy Wiener Roast

Build a hot charcoal fire in a large grill. Slit each wiener down the middle, insert a thin strip of cheese, and spiral a strip of thin bacon around the wiener. Secure the bacon with toothpicks or skewers. Grill over hot coals, turning as needed with tongs, until the bacon is ready to eat. Because these dogs drip lots of grease on the fire, they should be moved about on the grill to avoid fires. It's best to have a large surface area. When the dogs are almost ready to eat, sprinkle them lightly with Hungarian paprika. These can be eaten in a bun, but I like them on their own, served on a plate with lots of potato chips, baked beans, and other go-withs.

Variation: These dogs can also be baked or broiled. In either case, remember that the bacon will drip grease. I use a broiling pan as a grease catcher, fitted with a rack for holding the dogs.

✐ Corn Dogs

At fairs and other jubilees, corn dogs are often served on sticks. If you choose to use wooden skewers in this recipe, cook the corn dogs first, then insert the sticks. (If you are feeding children or your good ol' boys have been drinking, it's best to use a skewer without a sharply pointed end.) The large cookers and fish fryers heated by bottled gas make it easy to deep-fry these for outdoor events.

    1 pound 6-inch hot dogs
    1 cup fine stone-ground yellow cornmeal
    1 cup flour
    ¾ cup milk
    1 chicken egg, whisked
    2 tablespoons sugar
    2 tablespoons lard or vegetable shortening
    ½ tablespoon baking powder
    salt, to taste
    cooking oil for deep-frying

Rig for deep-frying, heating the oil to 350 degrees F. Mix the cornmeal, flour, sugar, salt, and baking powder in a bowl. Cut in the lard, mixing until the mixture forms crumbs. Stir in the milk and egg. Insert wooden skewers into the end of each hot dog and dip into the batter. Deep-fry the hot dogs, a few at a time, for 3 to 5 minutes, or until nicely browned. Drain. Serve with catsup and mustard.

Texas Wieners

In *The Only Texas Cookbook,* Linda West Eckhardt says that this sausage can be stuffed into ¾-inch casings (probably goat, she says) and be called wieners; or it can go into 1½-inch casings and be called knockwurst. The recipe below has been adapted from the book—but I choose to call them Texas Wieners.

    4 pounds lean beef
    4 pounds lean pork

2 pounds fatty bacon ends

1 cup minced onion

10 cloves garlic, minced

5 tablespoons salt

2 tablespoons ground coriander

4 teaspoons sugar

2 teaspoons ground mace

2 cups cold water

sheep, goat, or hog casings

Chop the meats and fat into chunks suitable for grinding. Mix the chunks well and spread them out on your work surface. Mix the salt, sugar, coriander, and mace; sprinkle evenly over the meats. Grind with a ¼- or ³⁄₁₆-inch plate. Grind again with a ⅛-inch plate. Mix in the onion, garlic, and water. Stuff into sheep casings (or goat) for regular wieners or into hog casings for jumbos, tying off in 6-inch lengths. Place the stuffed sausages into a pot, cover with water, bring to a boil, and simmer for 10 minutes. Drain. Refrigerate until cooking time, or freeze. To cook, prick the sausages with a needle, then grill, broil, poach, steam, or bake. Be sure to try these on a grill, perhaps beside chicken, lamb chops, or beefsteaks.

Italian Salami

Here's a recipe for a rather dry Italian-style salami, seasoned mostly with white pepper and a few red pepper flakes. It's my favorite for topping a cracker or, when thinly sliced, for helping fill a submarine or other sandwich. Note, however, that this sausage is not cooked. People who are bothered by this fact should know that jerky, gravlox, caviar, prosciutto, and ceviche are not cooked either. Anyone who prefers a fully cooked salami for noshing fare is encouraged to see the next recipe and Larry's Four-Day Venison Salami in Chapter 17.

6 pounds pork butt (certified)

4 pounds beef

2 cups dry red wine

15 cloves garlic, minced

8 tablespoons salt

4 tablespoons sugar

2 tablespoons whole white peppercorns

2 tablespoons ground white pepper

1 to 2 tablespoons crushed red pepper

beef casings (middles)

Cut the meat into chunks suitable for grinding. Spread the chunks out in a plastic tray, sprinkle evenly with the salt, cover, and refrigerate for 3 days. Spread the cured meat out over your work surface and sprinkle evenly with the sugar, crushed red pepper, and ground white pepper. (Hold the peppercorns.) Grind the mix with a 3⁄16-inch plate. Mix in the peppercorns, minced garlic, and wine. Stuff into beef casings, linking every 6 to 10 inches. Hang in a cool, dry place for 10 to 14 weeks, depending on the diameter of the salami. During the drying process, the salami will lose 30 to 40 percent of its weight. A few days of cold-smoking, if desired, should be considered part of the drying time. After drying, no mechanical refrigeration is required if the sausage can be hung in a cool, dry place. The links can, of course, be stored in the refrigerator or frozen.

If you want to cook the salami before eating, use it in fully cooked recipes or, for sandwiches and cracker snacks, simmer it in water for about 15 minutes per inch of thickness. Slices, of course, can be cooked quicker.

Variations: If you want to use a cure in addition to the salt, add 2 teaspoons of Prague Powder 1 or saltpeter mix, discussed in Chapter 3, being certain to mix the cure thoroughly into the salt. The cure mixes using sodium nitrate, sodium nitrite, or saltpeter will give the salami a redder color.

Submarine with Salami

Also called the poor boy, this great American sandwich was invented during the Great Depression at a wharf restaurant in New Orleans. Typically, it is made with slices of sandwich meats and cheeses. Although the original was probably made with sliced roast beef and ham, I can't imagine it without salami and thinly sliced tomato! The bread should be a whole small loaf, 8 inches or longer, on the chewy side.

sliced salami

sliced bologna

sliced ham or turkey

sliced Swiss cheese

sliced American cheese

thinly sliced onion

thinly sliced tomato

thinly sliced red bell pepper

thinly sliced green bell pepper

subway loaf

shredded lettuce

prepared mustard

mayonnaise

sliced olives

sliced pickled pepper (optional)

oil and vinegar (optional)

salt and freshly ground black pepper

Cut off the top part of the bread loaf. Spread mayonnaise and mustard on the bottom. Sprinkle on a layer of lettuce. Add overlapping slices of salami and other sandwich meats. Overlap a layer of Swiss and American cheese. Top with a layer of tomatoes, onions, bell peppers, olives, and, if desired, pickled hot peppers. Sprinkle with salt and freshly ground pepper, then drizzle on a little oil and vinegar, if desired. Replace the top part of the roll. Enjoy. This is a complete meal.

Hot-Smoked Salami

This salami is lightly smoked and fully cooked. Be sure to try it in sandwiches.

6 pounds beef

4 pounds pork butt

2 cups ice water

6 tablespoons salt

6 cloves garlic, minced

2 tablespoons whole white peppercorns

1 tablespoon freshly ground black pepper

1 tablespoon ground coriander

1 tablespoon ground cardamom

1 tablespoon ground mace

beef casings

Cut the meats into chunks suitable for grinding. Mix all the dried spices and seasonings; sprinkle evenly over the meats. Grind with a ³⁄₁₆-inch plate. Grind again with a ⅛-inch plate. Mix in the ice water and garlic. Stuff into beef casings. Cold-smoke for 1 to 2 hours, then increase the heat in the smokehouse to 170 degrees F. Hot-smoke for several hours, or until the internal temperature of the salami reaches 150 degrees F. Rinse in hot water, then dry and refrigerate for 12 hours or so before serving. This salami will keep for several days in the refrigerator. Freeze for longer storage.

Beef Salami

This all-beef salami, lightly smoked, is not cured. It can be eaten without cooking, but see the introduction to Italian salami, above.

8 pounds lean beef

2 pounds beef fat

1 cup dry red wine

6 cloves garlic, minced

6 tablespoons salt

2 tablespoons whole white peppercorns

1 tablespoon ground white pepper

1 tablespoon ground coriander

1 tablespoon sugar

1 teaspoon freshly ground black pepper

beef casings (middles)

Cut the meat and fat into chunks suitable for grinding, sprinkle evenly with the salt (keeping the lean and fat separate), spread the chunks out in a plastic tray, cover, and refrigerate for 3 days. Spread the lean meat out over your work surface and sprinkle evenly with the ground white pepper, black pepper, sugar, and coriander. (Hold the peppercorns.) Grind the mix with a ⅛-inch plate. Then grind the fat with a ¼-inch plate. Combine the meat and fat, mixing in the white peppercorns, minced garlic, and wine. Stuff into beef casings, linking every 6 to 10 inches. Cold-smoke for several hours, then hang in a cool, dry place for 8 to 10 weeks, depending on the diameter of the salami.

Slice this salami thinly for cold cuts, snacks, and sandwiches, or use it in recipes for dishes that call for salami. It can be fully cooked by steaming or by simmering in water for about 15 minutes per inch of diameter.

Variation: Add 2 teaspoons of saltpeter cure (Chapter 3) and omit an equal amount of salt. Thoroughly mix the cure with the rest of the salt before curing the meat.

Calabrese Salami

This highly spiced, hot salami is from the Calabria region of southern Italy. Be warned that the recipe is quite hot; you may want to cut back on the red pepper flakes, or, better, use some mild red pepper flakes.

10 pounds pork butt (certified)
1 cup brandy
1 cup vermouth
10 cloves garlic, minced
8 tablespoons salt
3 to 6 tablespoons hot red pepper flakes
2 tablespoons whole white peppercorns
1 tablespoon crushed dried fennel
beef casings or large hog casings

Cut the meat into cubes suitable for grinding. Sprinkle with salt, put into a plastic tray, cover, and refrigerate for 48 hours. Spread the meat out, sprinkle with the dried seasonings, and grind with a 3/16-inch plate. Mix in the garlic, brandy, and vermouth. Stuff into casings, dry, and hang in a cool place for 8 to 10 weeks.

Variation: Add 2 teaspoons of saltpeter cure (Chapter 3) and omit an equal amount of salt. Thoroughly mix the cure with the rest of the salt before curing the meat.

Bologna

This old sausage originated during the fifteenth century in Bologna, Italy. Since then, it has spread over the world. Today, it is usually made with part pork and part beef mixed with ice or ice water. The water helps give it a fine texture. The texture of modern-day market bologna can be approximated at home by more or less emulsifying the meat in a food processor. But you may prefer bologna made the old-fashioned way. I do.

6 pounds lean beef

4 pounds fatty pork (butt will do)

4 cups ice water

6 tablespoons salt (divided in half)

2 tablespoons white pepper

1 teaspoon ground coriander

1 teaspoon ground mace

beef round casings or muslin bags

Cut the beef into cubes and grind it with a ½- or ⅜-inch plate. Sprinkle it with about half the salt and cure it in a cool place for 2 days. Cut, grind, and salt-cure the pork for 2 days. Mix the cured meats on your work surface. Thoroughly mix all the dried spices, then sprinkle the mix over the meats. Grind the meats with a ⅛-inch plate. If a ³⁄₁₆-inch plate is the smallest you have, grind it twice. Slowly add the ice water, working the mixture with your hands as you go. Continue to work the mixture until it becomes rather sticky to the touch. This may take 30 minutes. Stuff the mixture into beef rounds or muslin bags, making fat links about a foot long. Hang the links overnight in a cool place. Heat some water to a boil in a large pot. Simmer (not boiling) on low heat for 30 minutes, or until the internal temperature of the center of the sausage reaches 150 to 160 degrees F. (Some experts say to cook it until it squeaks when pressed and released with your finger. I think the thermometer is more reliable.) Immerse the links into ice-cold water, hang to dry, and refrigerate. This bologna will keep for a week in the refrigerator. Freeze it for longer storage. Being precooked, it can be sliced and used for sandwich meat, or it can be cooked again in recipes. I like to thick-slice and grill, broil, or panfry it.

Variations: If you want to smoke-flavor the bologna, do so immediately after it is stuffed, using a cold smoke (less than 100 degrees F). Then cook it in the boiling water, cool, dry, and refrigerate. For another variation, mix 1 to 2 cups of grated onion with the meat before stuffing.

Smoked Beef Bologna

10 pounds good beef (such as chuck)

1 cup sugar

4 tablespoons salt

2 tablespoons white pepper

½ tablespoon freshly ground black pepper

1 tablespoon ground coriander

10 cloves garlic, minced

3 cups ice water

beef or large hog casings

Cut the beef into cubes, sprinkle with the salt and sugar, and refrigerate for 24 hours. Spread the beef out on your work surface and sprinkle evenly with the white pepper, black pepper, coriander, and minced garlic. Grind with a ⅜-inch plate. Grind again with a ⅛-inch plate. (Or grind twice with a ³⁄₁₆-inch plate.) Mix in the ice water, working the mix with your hands. Stuff the mixture into beef rounds or large hog casings. Dry and cold-smoke for 2 or 3 hours. Plunge into a large pot of hot water. Simmer at about 200 degrees F (do not boil) for an hour or longer, or until the internal temperature of the bologna reaches 150 degrees F. Hang to dry the surface, then refrigerate or freeze.

Liverwurst

This sausage should be more of a sandwich spread or cracker snack than a sliceable product. As such, it is packed into large casings and scooped out with a spoon or other utensil. There are many recipes, often calling for drastically different ratios of liver to pork. The measures below are about average. If you really like liver, add more and reduce the pork by an equal amount. If you don't like liver, maybe you're looking at the wrong recipe.

> **6 pounds pork butt**
> **4 pounds hog liver**
> **2 cups grated onion**
> **5 tablespoons salt, plus additional**
> **2 tablespoons sugar**
> **1½ tablespoons ground white pepper**
> **1 teaspoon ground sage**
> **1 teaspoon ground nutmeg**
> **1 teaspoon ground ginger**
> **beef casings (middles)**

Cut the pork into chunks, put it into a pot, cover with water, bring to a boil, and simmer for 30 minutes. Drain. Cut the liver into chunks and simmer it for 10 or 15 minutes. When cool, combine the pork and liver, mixing evenly on a work surface. Sprinkle evenly with the salt, spices, and onion. Grind with a ⅛-inch plate, or twice with a ³⁄₁₆-inch plate. Stuff into beef middles or large synthetic casings, tying off in 4-inch connected links. Put the links into some salted water in a large pot or oblong cooker. Bring to a boil, reduce the heat, and simmer for about 20 minutes. Put the links into cold water until they cool down, dry, and refrigerate until needed. It will keep for a week or so in the refrigerator. To freeze, separate the links and wrap in foil.

See also mettwurst, Chapter 6.

A. D.'s Cracker Spread

Spoon out some liverwurst and mix in some mayonnaise, mashing with a fork. Taste and adjust. To eat, spread a little of the mix on a cracker, top with a thin slice of Vidalia onion, and enjoy.

Pepperoni

One would think that this widely known sausage would have an ancient beginning. But the *pepper* part of the name comes from capsicum sorts, unknown to the Old World until Columbus discovered the New. Pepperoni as we know it today is flavored with either flakes of dried red pepper or powdered cayenne, or both, and is colored with another capsicum—mild paprika. Most pepperoni is rather small in diameter, partly because it is dried or semi-dried and partly because it is stuffed into rather small casings. Small hog casings are just right.

6 pounds pork butt

4 pounds beef

2 cups red wine

6 tablespoons salt

2 tablespoons sugar

1 tablespoon cayenne

1 to 2 tablespoons crushed red pepper flakes

1 tablespoon crushed anise seed

4 cloves garlic, minced

small hog casings

Cut the pork and beef into chunks suitable for grinding, sprinkle evenly with salt, and toss to coat all sides. Put the meats loosely in a plastic tray, cover, and refrigerate for 48 hours. Spread the meats, mixing them well, over a work surface. Sprinkle evenly with the dried seasonings. Grind the meats with a $\frac{3}{16}$-inch plate. Mix in the garlic and wine. Stuff into small hog casings, linking every 10 inches. Hang to dry in a cool place (34 to 40 degrees F) for 6 to 10 weeks. When dry, wrap each link in plastic film and keep refrigerated. It will keep for 2 or 3 months. Freeze for longer storage.

Note: If you want to use a cure, Chapter 3, substitute 2 teaspoons of it for an equal amount of the salt. Mix thoroughly with the salt before sprinkling the meat.

All-Beef Pepperoni

Follow the recipe above, using 10 pounds beef, 8 tablespoons salt,

3 tablespoons black pepper, 1 tablespoon crushed red pepper flakes, 1 tablespoon mustard seed, 1 tablespoon crushed fennel seed, 1 tablespoon anise seed, 10 minced cloves garlic, and 2 cups red wine. This recipe makes a very dry pepperoni, so you may want to shorten the drying period or substitute some beef fat for part of the meat.

Poultry and Wildfowl Sausages

G round turkey or chicken meat can be used in many of the recipes set forth in this book, with a few modifications. First, remember that chicken meat contains not much fat marbled in the flesh. A sausage made with chicken that has been skinned and trimmed of fat will be on the dry side. You can add some pork fat, or some fat and skin from the chicken.

Because of the salmonella problem with supermarket birds—birds raised, slaughtered, shipped, and stored in large batches—I believe it is best to raise and slaughter your own birds, or to hunt. I believe it strongly. Yet no one can deny the increasing popularity of chicken sausages and sandwich meats in our supermarkets and delis.

In addition to chicken and turkey, duck, goose, pheasant, ostrich, rhea, emu, and other birds can be used in sausage. Texture and content are usually more important than flavor, assuming, of course, that the birds have been properly dressed. Here's a brief guide, followed by some recipes for more commonly available birds.

Pheasant. Lean and dry. When used with 20 to 30 percent pork fat or suet, they produce a good sausage.

Partridge. It's hard to get up a large batch of partridge these days, but they do make good sausage, along with grouse, sage hens, and so on. Some of these birds can have a strong flavor; skinning will help. If you are lucky enough to have plenty of birds, make yourself some königswürste, a German creation composed of equal parts partridge and chicken, along with some chopped mushrooms and truffles, chicken eggs, salt, pepper, mace, and Rhine wine, all stuffed in large pork casings.

Ostrich. These large birds are now being raised in this country and other parts of the world. This good red meat is quite lean, although the bird contains lots of fat. Since these birds run instead of fly, the breast doesn't contain much meat, but the thighs do. Ostrich can be purchased in some meat markets and by mail order. Use it in sausage recipes like beef, or experiment with it in almost any recipe that calls for beef, pork, or veal. For texture, I recommend 80 percent lean meat and 20 percent fat.

I predict that sausages made with ostrich will become more common if the meat catches on with the American public. The bird yields lots of fat, and processors need a good way to use it.

Emu and Rhea. The Australian emu is similar to ostrich and is being raised commercially. Rhea, which is still hunted in Argentina, is also being raised, but it is smaller and may not be economically viable. Both have good red meat and should be used like ostrich.

Ducks and Geese. The rich, dark meat of the domestic duck is quite dry, although the skin is usually high in fat. Wild ducks and coot are also quite lean, and usually the skin doesn't contain as much fat. Either wild or domestic ducks make excellent sausage. (Some of the wild birds, however, have a strong flavor if they have been feeding heavily on fish, in which case they should be skinned.) Geese have similar meat and can be used in the same way as duck. Since geese grow for a long time, some of them are quite old and tough, in which case sausage makes a good way to use them.

Chicken Sausage

The ingredient list below is for whole chicken, including the skin and fat. If you use lean breast meat, add some pork or beef fat.

10 pounds chicken with skin and natural fat (or 7 pounds lean chicken and 3 pounds pork fat)

2 tablespoons salt

1 tablespoon freshly ground black pepper

1 tablespoon red pepper flakes

1 tablespoon dried sage

1 tablespoon dried thyme

1 tablespoon ground allspice

hog or sheep casings

Cut the chicken and skin (or pork fat) into chunks suitable for grinding. Spread the chunks on your work surface, sprinkle evenly with the salt and spices, and grind with a ⅛- or ³⁄₁₆-inch plate. Grind a small amount, shape into a patty, and fry it in a skillet to test for seasonings. Adjust the seasonings if necessary. Grind the whole batch and stuff into casings, linking every 4 inches or so. Cook right away or freeze. To cook, sauté in peanut or olive oil until cooked thoroughly and nicely browned. These can also be grilled, but make sure they are well done before serving. If in doubt, insert a meat thermometer into the center of the sausage. It should read at least 160 degrees F.

Variations: Turkey can be used instead of chicken. If so, try 7 pounds of turkey and 3 pounds of pork fat unless you want a very dry sausage.

French Chicken Sausage

The French make several sausages with chicken, and I find this one to be very easy to make because it uses cooked birds, which are very easy to bone and grind. To make it, I normally use chicken quarters that are on sale. I also use bacon ends and fresh or fresh frozen livers. To cook the chicken, I put it into a large pot of boiling water (heated by my bottle gas outdoor cooker) and add a few bay leaves, chopped celery, carrots, and some red pepper flakes. Normally, I cook about 20 pounds of leg quarters, bone out enough to make 8 pounds for the sausage, and save the rest for sandwich meat or chicken salad. After boning all the meat, I crack the bones, put them back into the stock, and simmer, covered, for an hour or so. Strain the broth, measure out 2 cups for the sausage, and save the rest for any recipe that calls for chicken broth. I usually freeze it in 1-cup containers. To cook the bacon and livers, use a smaller pot and cook them in simmering water for about 20 minutes.

8 pounds boned chicken, cooked
2 pounds chicken livers, cooked
2 pounds bacon ends, cooked
2 cups bread crumbs
2 cups chicken broth
12 large chicken eggs
3 tablespoons salt
1½ tablespoons white pepper
½ tablespoon ground clove
½ tablespoon ground nutmeg
sheep casings

Cook the chicken, livers, and bacon by the directions given in the introduction above. Chill the cooked meats, mix, and spread out over your work surface. Sprinkle the spices evenly over the mixture. Grind with a ³⁄₁₆-inch plate. Using your hands, mix in the eggs, bread crumbs, and chicken stock. Stuff into sheep casings, tying off in 6-inch links. To cook, panfry in butter or olive oil. Or, baste with olive oil and grill or broil.

Variation: This recipe makes an excellent way to deal with left-over turkey. I once tried it with about 6 pounds of leftover turkey, 2 pounds of leftover cooked fresh ham, 2 pounds of bacon ends, and 2 pounds of chicken livers purchased and boiled especially for the sausage recipe. Of course, the leftovers can be frozen and later thawed and made into sausage.

Italian Chicken or Turkey Sausage

Both chicken and turkey make excellent mild Italian sausages, lightly spiced. These can be used as patties or stuffed into small hog casings.

8 pounds lean chicken or turkey

2 pounds chicken fat, pork fat, or bacon

5 cloves garlic, minced

2 tablespoons salt

1 tablespoon cracked fennel seed

1 tablespoon freshly ground black pepper

small hog casings

Cut the meat and fat into chunks suitable for grinding. Mix and spread the chunks out on your work surface. Sprinkle evenly with the spices. Grind with a 3/16-inch plate. Stuff into hog casings, linking every 4 or 5 inches, or shape into patties. Cook right away or freeze. To cook, sauté the patties or links in olive oil until well done and nicely browned.

Hot Turkey Sausage

Similar to a fresh pork chorizo, this turkey sausage is just the ticket to spice up soups and stews, or, when sautéed, to serve with a bland boiled pozole (whole hominy) and sliced vine-ripened tomatoes.

7 pounds lean turkey meat

3 pounds pork fat or bacon

10 cloves garlic, minced

½ cup brandy

¼ cup dry red wine

¼ cup red wine vinegar

3 tablespoons salt

1½ tablespoons coarsely ground black pepper

1 tablespoon crushed red pepper

Spanish (hot) paprika, to taste

¾ tablespoon crushed fennel seed

½ tablespoon ground coriander

½ tablespoon ground allspice
medium hog casings

Cut the turkey meat and fat into chunks suitable for grinding, mixing and spreading the chunks out on your work surface. Mix all the dry spices and garlic and sprinkle evenly over the meat. Grind with a ⅛-inch plate. With your hands, mix in the red wine, brandy, and red wine vinegar. Stuff into hog casings, linking every 4 inches or so. To cook, sauté in olive oil until nicely browned and cooked through. Also, prick the links with a fork and use whole in soups and stews. These should be cooked right away or frozen.

Note: Wild turkey can also be used. It is better, really, because the meat is not as dry.

Fresh Ostrich Sausage

Speculating on ostrich farms has received lots of media attention in recent years, but how well the meat will be accepted by the American people remains to be seen. Marketing, not farming, may be the big problem. In any case, the meat is excellent and can be used in sausages. I think that it, like beef, works best with a mixture of rather fatty pork.

5 pounds ostrich thigh meat
5 pounds pork butt
4 tablespoons salt
2 tablespoons freshly ground black pepper
1 teaspoon dried sage
1 cup cold water
1 cup red wine
hog casings

Cut the meat into chunks suitable for grinding, spread out over your work surface, and sprinkle evenly with the dry seasonings. Grind with a ³⁄₁₆-inch plate. Mix in the wine and cold water. Stuff into hog casings. Refrigerate for a day or two, cook, or freeze. To cook, simmer the sausage for 15 or 20 minutes. Then fry or grill over charcoal until nicely browned and cooked through.

Variations: Emu and rhea can be used instead of ostrich.

Duck Sausage

The domestic duck sold in most American meat markets is billed as duckling. It usually contains lots of fat in the skin or connected to it, and I recommend using it in this recipe. A mix of 20 to 25 percent pork fat to 80 to 75 percent lean duck will also work, but note that duck skin is very good. I like to make cracklings of the duck skin—and I use the rendered oil for stir-fry.

If you raise your own ducks, or have access to such birds, by all means use them. In any case, it's best to bone the easy parts of the meat—breast, thigh, and perhaps the leg—and save the rest for duck soup or stock.

10 pounds duck, with skin and fat

½ cup dry red wine

3 tablespoons salt

2 tablespoons white pepper

2 teaspoons mustard seed

1 teaspoon freshly ground black pepper

1 teaspoon dried minced sage

½ cup minced onion

hog casings

Pluck the birds, bone out the meat with skin attached, cut into chunks, and spread out over your work surface. Mix all the dry ingredients and sprinkle evenly over the meat chunks. Grind with a ³⁄₁₆-inch plate. Mix in the wine and minced onion. Stuff into hog casings, linking every 6 inches or so. Hang in a cool, airy place just long enough to dry the surface of the casings, then cook, refrigerate, or freeze. To cook, prick the links with a fork and sauté in butter until nicely browned and cooked through. These can also be grilled over charcoal.

Wild Duck Variation: The meat from wild ducks can be used in the recipe above, adjusting for fat content. Some wild ducks have a strong rather fishy flavor, which is usually concentrated in the skin. For this reason, skin the ducks unless you are certain of their diet. When skinning the bird, look for shot holes, then remove any lead or steel shot. When cutting the meat into chunks prior to grinding, remove any shot or bloodshot areas. Once you get past the hemming and hawing, you'll find the wild duck one of the best meats. Be sure to save the bony pieces for soup or stock.

Note: If in doubt about using duck meat, try substituting it with an equal amount of veal, beef, or pork in your favorite sausage recipe. Also see the wonderful French recipe on page 112, which calls for duck, veal, and pork.

Venison and Game Sausages

I f you'll close your eyes and disengage any preconceived taste buds when sampling sausages made with various meats, it's the texture and fat content that make the difference. When making sausage, the tenderness of the meat isn't of prime importance; it's the leanness of the meat mixture that makes the sausage hard and tough. It follows that any good game or exotic meat can be used, along with some fat, to make good sausage.

There is, however, a big "if." The so-called "gamy" flavor of most wild meats comes about because the animal is improperly butchered, and the same taste will be found in a pig that is run all over the country with dogs, shot, and hauled back home on the hot hood of a pickup truck. Also, even prime game must be promptly gutted and cooled. The real reason for prompt field dressing is to remove the heat that the innards contain and open the body cavity to promote cooling.

Often meat from prime venison isn't fit to eat because of improper handling, and there is nothing you can do with it to make it tasty. Although sausage, usually being highly spiced, might seem to be a good way out, it really isn't. You simply can't make good sausage from bad meat, and, believe me, people have given me sausage that I couldn't eat. The unfortunate part here is that the characteristic taste has, over the ages, been termed "gamy," partly tainting all game in some people's minds.

In any case, game meat is widely available these days. One of the best animals—the white-tailed deer—is a downright nuisance in some areas of town and country. More and more, venison, buffalo, ostrich, alligator, freshwater turtle, and so on are available in special markets and by mail order. All of these meats can be made into good sausage. Most of these meats are on the lean side and, consequently, are better with the addition of fat.

When buying game or exotic meat for sausage, I recommend that you look for large chunks. It's true that the meat is often available in stew or ground form, but it's really best to grind your own. Freshly ground meat is not only better but is also safer, as a rule. If you butcher your own game, I would suggest that you reduce the meat to chunks suitable for stew meat or for grinding, then freeze it in 1-pound packages. Then you can use the meat for stews or ground for sausage, burgers, and so on. The 1-pound units permit you to get out exactly what you'll need, and the smaller units will be easy (as compared with a whole ham) to fit into the freezer and quicker to thaw. Remember that partly frozen meat is also easier to grind.

There are hundreds of good meats eaten in the modern world and I have eaten more than my share, including musk ox and lion. The list below is only an appetizer.

Bear. An excellent source of sausage meat, the black bear is hunted in several states. Other bears are also good, but legal hunting may be a problem. The meat is sometimes fatty, and the fat can be used in the sausage. Bear can carry trichinosis and should be cooked well done, or "certified" by freezing, as discussed in Chapter 1.

Whitetail and Other Deer. All deer, or venison, is quite lean as compared with beef. The fat in these animals—usually layered between the skin and the meat—is usually discarded, possibly because it is unpleasantly tallowy when cold or warm. Pure venison can be used for sausage, but I recommend a mixture of half venison and half fatty pork.

Elk. This large deer has dark meat similar to lean beef. It can be used instead of beef in many sausage recipes. In Siberia, a variety of elk is bred on farms and is an important source of meat.

Boar and Wild Pig. Unriled European boar as well as feral hogs can make excellent sausages, used as lean pork. Proper handling—a quick kill, prompt field dressing, and cooling of the meat—is essential. I've got at hand a book on how to dress game. In the case of boar, it says to scald the animal in hot water, scrape off the hairs, and then skin it! Obviously, you don't need to both scrape and skin the animal. The choice is yours, depending partly on your equipment and the circumstances.

As a rule, the meat from both European boar and feral pigs will be a little tougher than domestic hogs, and sometimes the flavor will be better, depending in part on what they have been eating. European boar and feral pig can carry trichinosis and should be cooked well done, or "certified" by freezing, as discussed in Chapter 1.

Moose. Called elk in Europe, this large animal makes excellent sausage. Owing to its size and internal body heat, it should be gutted as soon as possible after the kill.

Caribou. Called reindeer in Europe, this excellent deer might have been man's first domesticated animal after the dog. The Lapps and some Siberians still herd reindeer on a more or less nomadic basis, and they are raised commercially in some parts. Try caribou meat in any sausage recipe that calls for beef.

Buffalo. Also called bison, this dark, rich meat makes wonderful sausage. Leaner than beef, it should be mixed with fatty pork or bacon for the best results. It is available in some markets and by mail order these days. The real buffalo—the African cape—the Asian water buffalo, and the various African buffalo also make good sausages, and they are being raised commercially in limited quantities.

Other Meats. Mountain lion, giraffes (the neck meat is highly prized), various antelopes, wild sheep and goats, alligators, aardvarks, and dozens of other large animals are either hunted in some areas or raised commercially. Called exotics, some of these meats are available from specialty markets and by mail order.

Horse is also an excellent sausage meat, but it is seldom eaten in the United States. The horse was at one time a very important source of meat to the steppe people of Eurasia.

Elk Sausage

Elk is usually quite lean but full of flavor. Use stew meat, shoulder, or any other cut, being sure to trim out the sinew before grinding. I use beef fat (suet) instead of pork. Talk to your butcher, or save up some fat from your T-bones.

7 pounds elk meat

3 pounds beef fat

6 cloves garlic, minced

3 tablespoons salt

2 tablespoons coarsely ground black pepper

½ tablespoon anise seed, crushed

½ cup red wine

hog casings

Cut the meat and fat into chunks. Mix and spread the chunks out on your work surface, sprinkle evenly with the dry spices, and grind with a ³⁄₁₆-inch plate. Mix in the wine and garlic, stuff into hog casings, and twist into 4- to 6-inch links. Refrigerate overnight, then cook or freeze. They are best when grilled over charcoal or wood coals, flavored with smoke from a few wood chips.

Herter's Wyoming Polish Sausage

I have seen this recipe in several publications. This version has been adapted from *Bull Cook and Authentic Historical Recipes and Practices,* by George Leonard Herter and Berthe E. Herter. The recipe calls for 34 pounds of meat, but this isn't too much if you've got a mule deer or elk that needs reducing. Be sure to chill the meat before cutting and grinding it.

17 pounds mule deer (or other venison)

17 pounds lean fresh pork

12 ounces salt

8 ounces dried milk

1½ ounces freshly ground black pepper

1½ ounces ground sage

1½ ounces ground nutmeg

1 ounce ground ginger

½ ounce ground allspice

½ ounce Hungarian paprika

1 teaspoon garlic powder

4 ounces cold water

hog casings

Trim the meats, cut into chunks, mix, and spread out on your work surface. Mix all the dry ingredients, sprinkle evenly over the meats, and grind with a ³⁄₁₆-inch plate. Mix in the water with your hands. Stuff into hog casings, linking every 6 to 8 inches. Dry the casings and cold-smoke for 4 to 6 hours. (Herter says to use a low wood fire of maple, apple, mesquite, or hickory, and to smoke at about 120 degrees F. Colder smoke is better, I think.) Cook, refrigerate for several days, or freeze.

To cook Herter's Wyoming Polish Sausage, place the links in a skillet and add enough water to cover a third of them. Bring to a boil, lower the heat, cover, and simmer for 15 minutes. Pour the water out of the skillet, then increase the heat and fry until slightly browned on all sides. "Makes wonderful eating," Herter says. I agree.

These sausages can also be made into patties instead of links, seasoned with 2 teaspoons of Liquid Smoke. Try cooking the patties the same way as the link sausage, turning them carefully with a spatula.

Texas Venison Sausage

I have adapted this recipe from *The Only Texas Cookbook* by Linda West Eckhardt, who asked, "Is there a soul in Texas who hasn't been offered venison sausage at some time or other? In a state where deer are roughly the size of an aged jackrabbit, sausage making has come to be one of the prime products of the hunt. Some of the sausage is so bad that folks get real generous and want to give it away. I have tried everything from deer salami, which was dry, tough, and so strong it practically walked off the plate, to breakfast sausage so mild it was like eating hamburger. One of the best compromises I've found is a German links recipe, smoked to give it added resonance and containing saltpeter to retain a nice rosy color. If you object to nitrate, just leave the saltpeter out. The color will then be grayish. Don't be shocked at the quantity in this recipe. It assumes you just shot a deer."

14 pounds venison

7 pounds pork (80 percent lean)

1 cup noniodized table salt

⅓ cup coarsely ground black pepper

2 teaspoons saltpeter

hog casings

In the Texas book, the author said to mix the seasonings, sprinkle them over the meat, and grind once using a coarse blade. Then stuff into 1½-by-10-inch casings. I have altered the procedure a little. First, cut the meat into small chunks and sprinkle with the seasonings, being sure that the saltpeter is evenly mixed in with the salt and pepper. Put the meat into a plastic tray, cover, and refrigerate for 48 hours to cure the meat. Then grind, stuff, and hot-smoke slowly until the internal meat temperature reaches 160 degrees F. Cook right away or freeze until needed. To cook the sausage, place a link or two in a skillet with 3 tablespoons water, then "cover, cook, and turn until the water has evaporated and the sausage is an even brown color."

Larry's Four-Day Venison Salami

I have adapted this recipe from *The Bounty of the Earth Cookbook*, an excellent work by Sylvia Bashline. In addition to doubling the measures, I have changed the procedure a little, mostly to fit my way of grinding the meats. The recipe calls for beef suet, which is beef fat; if you don't have any, talk to your local butcher. Also, the recipe calls for red pepper. I use mild red pepper flakes, not cayenne. Suit yourself.

9 pounds venison

1 pound beef suet

12 teaspoons salt

5 teaspoons whole mustard seed

5 teaspoons freshly ground black pepper

5 teaspoons Liquid Smoke

4 teaspoons garlic powder

3 teaspoons mild red pepper flakes

Trim the venison, removing the sinew and fat. Cut the venison and suet into 1- to 2-inch chunks, mix them, and spread them out on a work surface. (Remember that partly frozen meat will be easier to cut and grind.) Mix the salt, mustard seed, black pepper, red pepper, and garlic powder. Sprinkle the mixture evenly over the meats. Drizzle the Liquid Smoke over the mix. Grind the meats. Mix with your hands, place in a nonmetallic container, and refrigerate overnight. Mix the meats every day for 3 days. On the fourth day, mix again and divide the mixture into 10 equal parts. Shape the parts into logs about 12 inches long. Place the logs on cookie sheets and bake at 155 degrees F for a total of 10 hours. After about 5 hours, turn the logs over. Remove the salami and roll each log in a paper towel. Wrap in foil and refrigerate until needed, for up to 3 weeks. For longer storage, wrap each log first in plastic foil and then in freezer paper. It will keep in the freezer for up to a year.

For noshing fare, slice the salami thinly and serve on crackers. Also, cut into slices for pizza and sandwiches, or in chunks for spaghetti sauce.

A. D.'s Easy Game Breakfast Sausage

It's no secret that I am fond of unusual meats, such as the emu. Hoping to introduce family and friends to such fare, I find that a mild breakfast sausage helps pave the way for medium-rare steaks. The ingredient list calls for venison—which can be from moose, elk, whitetail, mule deer, caribou, and so on—but any good fresh lean meat can be used. The ingredient list also calls for bacon ends. These are scraps left over from commercial bacon operations and as such are often sold in bulk quantities in supermarkets and meat markets at reduced prices. Regular bacon can be used. The list also calls for A. D.'s Basic Sausage Mix (Chapter 1). Use any commercial mix that you choose, or, better, come up with your own, starting with salt and pepper and, I insist, a little sage.

7 pounds lean game meat

3 pounds bacon ends

4 tablespoons A. D.'s Basic Sausage Mix (page 21)

Cut the meat and bacon into pieces suitable for grinding. Spread out over your work surface, sprinkle with about ¾ of the seasoning mix, and grind a little with a ³⁄₁₆- or ⅛-inch plate. Shape into a thin patty. Heat a little bacon grease or oil in a skillet, then fry the patty for a few minutes on each side, until just done and lightly browned. Taste and adjust seasonings if necessary. Grind the rest of the batch. Shape into patties and either cook or freeze. For freezing, I wrap each patty in plastic film. I find that it is not necessary to thaw the patties prior to frying, and that not much cooking oil will be needed. Thus, these patties make a quick and good breakfast when served with eggs or perhaps between biscuits—or both ways.

18

Fish Sausages

ish sausages may well be the rave of the future, and, it seems to me, ground meat and sausage make an ideal way to use fish that are difficult to market under their proper names, although they might well be better than more familiar fish. And using fish in sausage is not undreamed of in the past. Madrilene sausages, for example, according to my old edition of *Larousse Gastronomique*, are made with a mixture of veal, pork fat, and sardine fillets packed in oil. Made in small beef casings, these sausages are poached for 10 minutes in veal stock, then fried in butter. Sounds good, at least to me. Here are some other suggestions.

Bony Fish Sausage

Sausage is a very good way to use bony fish, most of which are really quite tasty. For this recipe I use chain pickerel because I catch lots of 'em, but any good fish with mild white flesh will do. Suckers are especially good, which may be a surprise to many people. Many writers claim to be able to "gash" bony fish in such a way that the meat can be eaten bones and all. (Of course, I'm talking about the small Y-shaped intermuscular bones, not the backbone or rib cage.) I've never figured out whether the fish should be gashed crosswise, lengthwise, or diagonally. So, I came up with my own way of dealing with the bones: (1) Fillet the fish and cut out the rib bones; (2) cut the fish lengthwise into ¾-inch strips; (3) then cut the strips into a ½-inch dice; and (4) grind the dice in a sausage mill with a ⅛-inch plate. By then, the bones are scarcely noticeable—except perhaps by someone looking for them.

Of course, you can use several kinds of fish in the same recipe in case you catch a mixed stringer.

10 pounds fish fillets
10 slices white bread
10 large chicken eggs
2 cups milk
½ cup chopped fresh parsley
2 tablespoons salt
2 teaspoons freshly ground black pepper
1 teaspoon cayenne
1 teaspoon dried sage
sheep casings

Shred the bread, discarding the brown edge, and soak in milk. Set aside. Dice the fillets as directed above. Mix in the salt, black pepper, cayenne, and sage. Grind with a ⅛- or ³⁄₁₆-inch plate. Mix in the milk, bread, parsley, and eggs. Shape a patty and fry it in a skillet. Taste for seasonings and test for bones. If needed, grind the mix again. Stuff the mixture into sheep casings or small hog casings. Cook, refrigerate for a day or two, or freeze. To cook, sauté the sausage in butter until nicely browned.

Note: This recipe is a variation of *Rabakozi Halkolbasz,* a Hungarian fish sausage. I don't have documentation for my hunch, but it seems probable that carp are used in Europe, as they are popular as table fare as well as for sportfishing.

Variations: Vary the seasonings to suit your taste or fancy. The fish will pick up on most any theme. Try mixed seasonings, such as Italian, Greek, or Cajun.

A. D.'s Skate Sausage Patties with Salsa

One of the best ways to cook skates and rays, in my opinion, is to grind them in a sausage mill, shape the meat into patties, and cook them on a griddle or skillet, or perhaps stuff them into medium hog casings. The sausage patties can be eaten between buns, or they can be eaten on a plate along with vegetables, rice, salad, and other parts of a complete meal. The recipe below has been adapted from my *Saltwater Fish Cookbook*.

The Patties

1 pound skate wings
bacon drippings
1 small-to-medium onion, chopped
salt and pepper, to taste
1 or 2 chicken eggs (if needed)
flour (if needed)
salsa (below)

Cut the skate into chunks and brush with bacon drippings. Peel and chop the onion. Mix the skate and onion, adding a little salt and pepper. Grind the mixture in a sausage mill, using a ⅛- or ³⁄₁₆-inch plate. Shape part of the mixture into a patty, handling it very carefully. Heat about 1 tablespoon of bacon drippings on a griddle or in a skillet, then cook the patties for about 5 minutes on each side, or until done, turning once. Do not overcook. If the patty has held together properly, proceed with the rest of the batch. But if the patty tears apart, you may need some binder to help hold things together. In this case, whisk a chicken egg or two and stir it into the sausage along with a little flour. When all of the patties have been cooked, top with salsa and serve hot.

The Salsa

¾ cup chopped tomato
¾ cup mango cubes (½-inch dice)
¾ cup finely chopped onion

183

¼ **cup red bell pepper**
¼ **cup green bell pepper**
¼ **cup chopped fresh cilantro**
2 **cloves garlic, minced**
1 **fresh jalapeño, seeded and minced**
1 **tablespoon olive oil**
1 **teaspoon fresh lemon juice**
½ **teaspoon salt**

Heat the oil in a skillet, then sauté the onion, peppers, garlic, and cilantro for 5 or 6 minutes. Stir in the rest of the salsa ingredients, then simmer for a few minutes. Keep hot until the sausage patties are cooked.

A. D.'s Gefilte Fish Sausage (not kosher)

According to *The Jewish Festival Cookbook* by Fannie Engle and Gertrude Blair, poached fish balls, like gefilte fish, are served up with dill pickles and a relish made of chopped beets and horseradish. When working on a magazine article a while back, I tried recipes for various mixes of ground fish shaped into balls and for gefilte, which is such a mixture stuffed into the skin of the fish. It didn't take much of a spark to expand on the theme. Hog casings may not be kosher but using them is a good deal easier than skinning a fish (for me the problem is how to keep the fish skin intact without making holes in it). I made the sausage with suckers and chain pickerel, a cousin to the northern pike, a fish often used in gefilte, along with carp. But any good fresh fish will do. You should, of course, make good use of the trimmings; that is, the head, fins, skin, and bony parts. These will be needed for the fish stock used to cook the sausage and as an ingredient in the sausage. Having an exact amount of fish isn't critical, but for best results I like to have about 4 pounds of undressed chain pickerel, suckers, or other good fish.

The Sausage

fillets from 4 pounds jacks
2 **medium carrots, diced**

2 medium onions, diced

2 chicken eggs

¼ cup matzoh meal

1 tablespoon olive oil

1 teaspoon ground sea salt

1 teaspoon sugar

fish stock (from the recipe below)

hog casings or sheep casings

Fillet, gash, and dice the fish exactly like those in the bony fish recipe (page 181). Mix the diced vegetables with the fish. Grind the fish and vegetables in a sausage mill, using a ⅛-inch plate. Using your hands, mix in the chicken eggs, matzoh meal, olive oil, sea salt, and sugar. Stuff the mixture into small hog casings or sheep casings, linking every 3 inches.

Heat the strained stock (recipe below) in a large electric skillet. Ideally, the stock should be just deep enough to cover the sausages. Add a little water if needed. Bring the broth to a boil, then reduce the heat. Add the sausages and simmer for 15 to 20 minutes. Serve these sausages directly from the electric skillet, which is used to keep them warm. Delicious.

Variations: If you have frozen fish fillets without the head and trimmings, use canned or homemade chicken stock instead of fish stock. Also, feel free to add more pepper and spices, or experiment with the vegetable ingredients. I want to point out, however, that the carrots give a nice color to this sausage.

The Stock

heads and trimmings from 4 pounds fish

2 medium carrots, diced

2 medium onions, diced

2 stalks celery with tops, diced

½ teaspoon ground cinnamon

salt and pepper, to taste

Put the fish parts into a pot, cover with water, and add the rest of the ingredients. Bring to a boil, cover, reduce the heat, and simmer for an hour or so. Strain the stock. Discard the remains, unless you want to gnaw on what's left of the fish heads, as I do.

Glossary

Age. To hang meat in a dry place after curing. If the meat has been properly cured, the temperature at which the meat is aged is not critical. Proper aging gives a distinct flavor to country hams and other meats, and sometimes to sausages.

Ascorbic acid. A form of vitamin C that is used in canning to preserve the color of fruits and vegetables. It is sometimes added to a meat cure to help retain the color of the meat or sausage. Some authorities plug this stuff for use in sausages; others don't.

Botulism. A deadly food poisoning that is usually caused by improper canning of meat, fish, and vegetables. It can develop in sausages. In order to reach dangerous levels, the spores, which produce a toxin, require moisture and a lack of oxygen. It may, however, occur in some cased sausages (made with meat that hasn't been salt-cured) and possibly in other moist meats. Some authorities say that the use of sodium nitrate, sodium nitrite, and saltpeter help prevent botulism in sausages and other meats. For proper use of these additives, see Chapter 3.

Casings. Cleaned sheep, hog, or cow intestines used to stuff sausages. When properly cleaned and salted, these can be kept for months and months in the refrigerator or longer in the freezer. They can be purchased, already salted, from sausage and meat supply houses. Artificial casings are also used these days. See also Chapter 3.

Certified pork. Uncured pork that has been frozen at a low temperature for a long time in order to negate any trichina—a microscopic worm found in hogs and bears. When ingested, it can cause serious illness. Fully cooking the meat kills trichina. See also Chapter 1.

Clostridium perfringens. Bacteria that can form a toxin if they are allowed to multiply in foods. These are inactive at temperatures below 40 degrees F and above 140 degrees F. Once the toxin develops, it cannot be destroyed by ordinary cooking. The toxin can, however, be avoided by properly handling the meat before, during, and after grinding. The bacteria are inhibited by salt, alcohol, acid, sugar, lack of moisture, and low temperatures.

Cold-smoking. Smoking meats or fish at a low temperature for a long period of time. The temperature should be below 100 degrees F, and preferably between 70 and 80 degrees F. Bacteria multiply rapidly at temperatures between 80 and 140 degrees F. Smoke itself does little to cure meat or prevent bacterial growth. The absence of moisture that goes along with many smoking operations retards the growth of moisture—a point that you should remember before using the water pan provided with some types of smokers.

Hot-smoking is really cooking with the addition of smoke for flavor. It should be accomplished at temperatures higher than 140 degrees F. See also the discussions in Chapter 3.

Country sausage. This popular term has no precise meaning, and I take it to mean the old-time sausages made on hog-killing day, usually in the fall of the year. There are thousands of recipes, but usually they are made with only a few ingredients and in America are likely to contain flaked red pepper and sage.

Cure. A brine or a dry mixture containing salt and sodium nitrite and possibly other ingredients. Salt is the critical element. The word *cure* is sometimes used to denote sodium nitrite, sodium nitrate, potassium nitrite, or potassium nitrate. As a verb, *cure* means simply "to cure." *Aging* has a separate meaning. Cured meats can be aged, in which case temperature is not as important as in curing.

Dry. To dry sausage by hanging in a cool, dry place for several weeks. Before drying, the sausage meat must be cured. See also Chapter 3.

Dry cure. A meat cure consisting of dry ingredients, mostly salt. As a verb, *dry-cure* means "to cure with dry ingredients." In home sausage making, the meat is usually cut into chunks, put into a plastic tray, sprinkled with the cure (or plain salt), covered, and placed in the refrigerator for about 2 days. (Note that cutting the meat into chunks cuts down on the time required to cure the meat. With larger chunks of meat, such as whole ham, salt penetration and salt equalization may take months.) After stuffing in casings, the sausage may or may not be dried.

Hot-smoking. Flavoring sausages or other foods with the aid of smoke during the cooking process. Hot-smoked sausages can be eaten immediately after the simultaneous cooking and smoking is over, but they are not cured or preserved.

Hygrometer. A device used to measure the humidity inside a meat-curing chamber. It can be important for commercial applications, where the exactness is important to duplicate results from one batch of sausage to another.

Kosher salt. A coarse salt that can be used for pickling and sausage making.

Liquid Smoke. A commercial product, widely available, flavored with real smoke. I seldom use it, but many others do. It can be added to many of the recipes in this book. When mixing the sausage, add 2 teaspoons per 10 pounds of meat.

Nitric oxide. When sodium nitrite is applied to meat, it breaks down into a chemical called nitric oxide, which is really the stuff that does the work.

Pickling salt. A salt that contains no iodine. It is sold commercially for use in pickling, canning, or meat curing or brining.

Potassium nitrate. Saltpeter. In the past, saltpeter has been widely used in meat cures and in gunpowder. At the time of this writing, it has been banned for use in commercially cured meats. See also Chapter 3.

Prague Powder. A trade name for a curing mixture of salt and chemicals. Prague Powder 1 contains salt and sodium nitrite. Prague Powder 2 contains salt, sodium nitrite, and sodium nitrate. See the discussion in Chapter 3.

Salmonella. Bacteria that can cause food poisoning. To reach dangerous levels in meats, they require moisture and the right temperature window. Salmonella is a problem especially with modern mass-produced poultry, although the bacteria can also multiply in other meat and fish, as well as in eggs. It is not a problem with sausages that have been properly cured and fully cooked. If in doubt about cooking fresh sausages, it's best to simmer the links in water for about 20 minutes. Then they can be dried to the touch and sautéed or grilled.

Salt. Sodium chloride. The term *curing salt* is sometimes applied to sodium nitrite and other chemicals. There are several kinds of salt, depending on how it is mined or processed. Of course, most salts are not pure sodium chloride. Any natural salt can be used for curing meats or making sausages.

It has been noted that man did not use sodium nitrite and other minerals in his cured meats until quite recently. This is not the whole story. Until recently, these minerals were not removed from natural sea salt before it was used for curing meats. Modern man is, in short, taking sodium nitrite and potassium nitrate and other minerals out of salt—and then putting them back into the salt used to cure meats.

In any case, my favorite salt for curing and table use is unrefined sea salt simply because it has a good flavor. Sea salt is, however, too expensive these days to use for large-scale meat curing.

Salt also comes in various grains, from fine to large chunks commonly known as ice cream salt. Any of the forms can be used in a brine, provided it is well mixed, but salts for dry cures work best in a fine grain. Regular table salt works just fine for making sausages.

Saltpeter. Potassium nitrate. It is used in meat curing and in explosives. Saltpeter is poisonous and should be used carefully in small amounts, if at all. It has been banned for use in commercial meats. It was, however, widely used in old-time home sausage recipes, and is still used extensively today. See also the comments in Chapter 3.

Sodium nitrate. A sodium-nitrogen salt that is widely used in meat cures as well as in fertilizer and explosives. Because it is toxic, sodium nitrate should be used carefully in small amounts and should be mixed thoroughly with salt. Both federal and state agencies limit the use of sodium nitrate in commercial meats. See also Chapter 3.

Sodium nitrite. A salt that is widely used in meat cures. Because it is toxic, sodium nitrite should be used carefully in small amounts and should be mixed thoroughly with salt. Both federal and state agencies limit the use of sodium nitrite in commercial meats. See also Chapter 3.

Staphylococcus aureus. Bacteria that can form a toxin if allowed to multiply in foods. These are inactive at temperatures below 40 degrees F and above 140 degrees F. Once the toxin develops, it cannot be destroyed by ordinary cooking. The toxin can, however, be avoided by properly handling the meat before, during, and after grinding. The bacteria are inhibited by salt, alcohol, acid, sugar, lack of moisture, and low temperatures.

Summer sausage. This term is loosely used. I use it to mean any sausage that is made in cold weather and intended to last into or perhaps through the summer. Usually, summer sausage is cured and dried.

Trichina. A microscopic worm found in hogs and bears. When ingested, it can cause serious illness. Fully cooking the meat kills trichina. Freezing will also kill the worm, as discussed in Chapter 1.

Sources of Materials and Supplies

Local meat processors and markets often sell sausage seasonings and casings as well as meats. Seasoning mixes, spices, and casings, as well as sausage equipment and supplies, can also be purchased by mail order. Here are some good sources.

Cumberland General Store, 1 Highway 68, Crossville, TN 38555. This mail-order firm publishes an interesting catalog, chock full of hard-to-find old-time items. They carry several hand-cranked sausage mills and stuffers, along with a complete line of spare parts and attachments. Spices, cures, and seasonings are also available, as are books, knives, etc. Their catalog is marketed in retail outlets, such as bookstores and magazine racks, at $4. If you order, the price of the catalog is redeemable with four $1 coupons, using one coupon for every $10. My local IGA grocery store discounts magazines 10 percent, so I came out 40¢ ahead on my $51 order. And I've still got the catalog, which I use for reference and nostalgic browsing into bygone days.

Grandma LaMure's Spice 'n' Slice, P.O. Box 26051, Phoenix, AZ 85068. If you want to make 2-pound batches of sausages without using a stuffer, try this firm's inexpensive no-fuss mixes. At present they offer packages for salami, bologna, pepperoni, jerky, country sausage, "southern sausage," and jerky. I have tried all the mixes with excellent results.

King Arthur Flour, P.O. Box 876, Norwich, VT 05055. Whole grains, buckwheat, and other ingredients.

Penzey's, Ltd., P.O. Box 1448, Waukesha, WI 53187. An excellent mail-order source for spices and seasonings. In addition to peppers, spices, and herbs, Penzey's also offers various sausage seasonings, including mixes for bratwurst, Italian sausage, venison sausage, Polish sausage, Russian sausage, and a breakfast sausage.

The Sausage Maker, Inc., 26 Military Road, Buffalo, NY 14207. Bulk spices, sausage spice mixes, meat cure mixes, sausage additives, and equipment for grinding, stuffing, drying, and smoking sausage. Some of the equipment is designed for the small manufacturer. I find the firm to be a reliable mail-order source for natural and artificial casings, including several sizes of salted hog, sheep, and cow gut.

Further Reading

Ashbrook, Frank G. *Butchering, Processing, and Preservation of Meat.* Van Nostrand Reinhold Company, New York, 1955.

Kutas, Rytek. *Great Sausage Recipes and Meat Curing.* The Sausage Maker, Inc., Buffalo, NY, 1984.

Livingston, A. D. *Cold-Smoking & Salt-Curing Meat, Fish, & Game.* Lyons & Burford, New York, 1995.

Predika, Jerry. *The Sausage-Making Cookbook.* Stackpole Books, Mechanicsburg, PA, 1983.

Reavis, Charles G. *Home Sausage Making.* Storey Communications, Inc., Pownal, VT, 1987.

Savic, I. V. *Small-Scale Sausage Production.* Food and Agriculture Organization of the United Nations, Rome, 1985.

Sleight, Jack. *The Complete Sausage Cookbook.* Stackpole Books, Mechanicsburg, PA, 1995.

Ubaldi, Jack, and Elizabeth Crossman. *Meat Book.* Macmillan Publishing Company, New York, 1987. This book has some excellent recipes for sausage, along with some strong opinions on the use of saltpeter, but its main focus is on the meat itself, especially pork, beef, lamb, veal, and poultry.

Index